The Democratic Differentiated Classroom

Sheryn Spencer Waterman

EYE ON EDUCATION
6 DEPOT WAY WEST, SUITE 106
LARCHMONT, NY 10538
(914) 833–0551
(914) 833–0761 fax
www.eyeoneducation.com

Library of Congress Cataloging-in-Publication Data
Waterman, Sheryn Northey.
The democratic differentiated classroom / Sheryn Spencer Waterman.
      p. cm.
   Includes bibliographical references.
   ISBN 1-59667-032-0
   1. Teaching—Philosophy. 2. Education—Aims and objectives. 3.
Motivation in education. 4. Education—Social aspects. 5.
   Student participation in administration. 6. Curriculum planning. 7.
   Classroom management. I. Title.
LB1025.3.W374 2006
371.2'52—dc22
                                        2006022437

   10 9 8 7 6 5 4 3 2 1

Editorial and production services provided by
Richard H. Adin Freelance Editorial Services
52 Oakwood Blvd., Poughkeepsie, NY 12603-4112
(845-471-3566)

Also Available from EYE ON EDUCATION

**Handbook on Differentiated Instruction
for Middle and High Schools**
Sheryn Spencer Northey

**Differentiated Instruction:
A Guide for Middle and High School Teachers**
Amy Benjamin

**Differentiated Instruction Using Technology:
A Guide for Secondary Teachers**
Amy Benjamin

**Differentiated Instruction:
A Guide for Elementary School Teachers**
Amy Benjamin

**The Four Most Baffling Challenges for Teachers:
And How to Solve Them**
Sheryn Spencer Waterman

**Differentiated Instruction:
A Guide for Foreign Language Teachers**
Deborah Blaz

**Classroom Motivation from A to Z:
How to Engage Your Students in Learning**
Barbara R. Blackburn

**Active Literacy Across the Curriculum:
Strategies for Reading, Writing, Speaking, and Listening**
Heidi Hayes Jacobs

**Seven Simple Secrets:
What the BEST Teachers Know and Do!**
Annette Breaux and Todd Whitaker

How to Reach and Teach ALL Students – Simplified
Elizabeth Breaux

**What Great Teachers Do Differently:
Fourteen Things That Matter Most**
Todd Whitaker

Meet the Author

Sheryn Spencer Waterman is the Gifted Specialist at Flat Rock Middle School in Western North Carolina. Her many accomplishments include "Teacher of the Year" in two schools, National Board Certification (1997), and Founding Fellow for the Teacher's Network Leadership Institute. She came to teaching after working for several years as a psychotherapist and consultant. She is a member of the Board of Trustees for the North Carolina Center for the Advancement of Teaching and has worked on several local, state, regional, and national projects to promote quality teaching. This is her third book on teaching.

Table of Contents

1

The Democratic Differentiated Classroom

The students in my eighth grade remedial reading class and I decided to have a party to celebrate the last days before a holiday break. We brought in food and drinks to share with each other. However, as class time was coming to an end, all the students in the class were so intensely engrossed in completing their projects for our unit that they were not interested in stopping to have a party!

These students had scored below normal on their state end-of-grade test. Based on those scores they were assigned to remedial reading. At the beginning of the year *none* of them wanted to be in the class. They were allowed to have laptop computers but were supposed to use those laptops to access a scripted reading program. After the novelty of having laptops wore off, so did their interest in doing the scripted reading program. I had to think of something.

I had recently read something that convinced me about the importance of allowing students choices; I decided to give it a try. I asked my students what *they* wanted to learn through reading. They wanted to read about topics of interest to *them* and they wanted to make PowerPoint presentations with lots of pictures and minimal words. I was amazed by the variety of their topics, which included pop stars, sports teams, favorite novels, shoes, and Santa Claus.

They also enjoyed seeing their work projected on the LCD projector. Displaying their work on the big screen enabled them to show off what they had created and increased their interest in making the work something of which they could be proud. Showing the class what they had created became more important to them than celebrating with a party.

In this class educational strategies and students' needs resonated with each other. It was a place without behavior or motivation problems. It was what education should be like on most days. When students will not quit doing their work to have a party, you know you have created a democratic differentiated classroom.

All of the examples related are fictionalized to protect the identity of my students and colleagues.

What Is "Democratic" About in the Democratic Differentiated Classroom?

The *democratic* differentiated classroom is based on ideas from several educational theorists and practitioners. It is primarily based on the work of John Dewey (1916), whose book *Democracy and Education* shows us the importance of preparing students to preserve our democratic nation. In the democratic classroom, the underlying belief is that students are members of a community in which responsibility for learning is *shared*. The teachers are not dictators; they share the responsibility of leading the class with the students. It also means that students have certain freedoms: freedom of speech, freedom to choose, and freedom to question the system. Teachers in the democratic classroom facilitate learning by guiding students toward using these democratic freedoms responsibly and with careful thought. They help students develop an understanding of metacognitive processes (learning about learning) that foster independent and lifelong learning.

This idea of democracy in the classroom is also based on the work of Jane Nelson (1996), who developed a discipline model from the work of Albert Adler (1870–1937) and Rudolf Dreikurs (1897–1972): the model is called *Positive Discipline*. In Nelson's model, the teacher is respectful of students' perspectives and shares with them the responsibility for the discipline in the classroom. The cornerstone of this model is "the classroom meeting" in which students discuss important classroom issues in a structured setting. The democratic classroom takes this idea of a class meeting one step further by asking students to use the meeting to determine aspects of the curriculum and aspects of classroom order.

Finally, the idea of a democratic classroom in which students "vote" is based on the work of Edward Deci (1995) and brain-based research (Jensen, 1998). Both Deci and brain-based researchers tell us that students are intrinsically motivated if they are given chances to make choices. Deci tells us to offer choices rather than telling students what is required. He says that if teachers present ideas as choices or if they side with the students' when it comes to issues about which they may have no choice, they will have very little trouble with student motivation. Additionally, brain-based researchers tells us that brains want to learn and that by allowing choice and the absence of threat, students will not require bribery or punishment to motivate them to learn. By allowing students the democratic process of voting on what they learn as often as possible, they will more likely accept responsibility for their education. If they want to be successful in the class, they will be more likely to accept those activities that are more difficult and that they may not be able to choose. For example, adult citizens of a democracy understand that their freedom is limited for the good of the society and that every citizen must do things they may not love to do (like paying taxes).

Unfortunately, many students *do* exercise their right to choose *not* to comply with nonnegotiable activities on a daily basis in our classrooms. These students refuse to do homework, refuse to take standardized tests, and refuse all bribery or punishment that is meant to motivate them to comply with our dictates. The democratic classroom offers an alternative to traditional methods of motivating students to achieve in our diverse classrooms.

What Is the "Differentiated" About in the Democratic Differentiated Classroom?

The *differentiated* aspect of this model also originates from the ideas of John Dewey who said that *teachers must align their instruction to meet the needs of their students*. More than ever before, we have a mandate to reach every student in our classrooms. No child must be left behind. Looking at dropout rates and the work of John Goodlad (2004) makes it impossible for educators to ignore the fact that current teaching practices are failing to meet the needs of far too many students.

In the early 1990s, Carol Ann Tomlinson gave structure to the idea of meeting the needs of all students when she proposed the "differentiated" classroom. She explained in her book, *How to Differentiate Instruction in the Mixed Ability Classroom*, that in order to meet the needs of all students, teachers must learn to address the issues of students' interests, learning styles, and readiness (or ability). Also, in order to be fair to all learners, teachers must plan lessons that provide various content, processes, and products that align with those interests, styles, and abilities.

Many educators have written books showing teachers how to differentiate instruction in their classrooms. I wrote a book called *Handbook on Differentiated Instruction for Middle and High School* (Northey, 2005) in which I gave a variety of ideas for differentiating instruction based on Carol Ann Tomlinson's frameworks and other ideas. I still use those ideas (1995); however, differentiation of instruction, especially in the upper grades can be difficult. If a teacher has 100 or 150 students, how can she know each one of them well enough to tailor her instruction to meet each one's needs? This question has not been answered thoroughly by the current literature; I have written this book to help teachers meet the needs of their students by using both the ideas: differentiation and democracy.

Implementing the Democratic Differentiated Classroom Model

The democratic differentiated classroom model is more easily implemented than prior models because it shifts to students, some of the responsibility for differentiation. This model utilizes the concepts proposed by Carol Ann Tomlinson, but makes it easier to implement the differentiated classroom for teachers at all levels. Asking students to choose standards-based activities based on their *self*-knowledge is superior to asking teachers to understand, at high levels, all the aspects of each student in order to plan differentiated instruction. If the teacher guides students' development of self-knowledge and helps students understand curriculum standards, the collaboration will create learning activities that are accessible and interesting for all students. The only difficult part of this process is that the teacher must risk giving up some control and be willing to trust that her students *can* make responsible decisions.

Why Choose This Model

In our present culture, we too often hear about young people who have made disastrous choices about how to live their lives. Many of these young people have chosen drugs and alcohol or lives of crime instead of productive and rewarding lives. Most young people learn to make good choices from their own parents, but too many lack the benefits of that kind of guidance. Schools have a major role in teaching students to make good choices about learning. We educators may not have not done enough to teach them this skill because we have not given them enough opportunities to practice choice making in the safe environment of our classrooms.

This model is not about giving students so much freedom that the classroom becomes chaotic. This is about teachers working beside students to hear their views and desires about learning and then helping them translate those views and desires into valuable skills, knowledge, and attitudes.

If students do not practice making good decisions about their education in schools, where will they learn to do this? Believing this kind of classroom can work is half the battle; the other half is making it work.

This Model Promotes Achievement

This democratic differentiated classroom model is not just theoretical. I have used this concept with highest and lowest performing students. I know it works for me as a teacher and I can tell by the fact that my students do their work, and do it well, that it works for them. Since I began using this model, I have written only two referrals to the office and **no students fail my class**. I will not say it is perfect. For instance, I still get some stories about dogs eating homework, but I eventually get all of the homework turned in (and I give lots of it).

Here is another example of how well the model has worked for me. I teach Language Arts; all students at my grade level take a state test of writing skills. After using this model, my students' writing scores helped our school gain the distinction of having the highest writing scores in our region.

Aligned with SCANS

One final consideration for choosing this model is that it is closely aligned with the skills and competencies students need to succeed in today's world. The U.S. Department of Labor and Education created the Secretary's Commission on Achieving Necessary Skills (SCANS) to determine these skills and competencies. The published report, *What Work Requires of Schools: A SCANS Report for America 2000,* has inspired educators to plan a school-to-work curriculum to address these competencies. The democratic differentiated classroom model fits the spirit of this document better than most because it is concept-based, it promotes group learning, and it shifts responsibilities for learning and performing onto the shoulders of students. (See "Skills and Competencies Needed to Succeed in Today's Workplace." Retrieved June 24, 2006.)

A Word of Caution

If you like this idea, you may want to implement it cautiously. You may want to carefully document to make sure you *are* guiding students' choices so that their learning activities address the achievement and behavioral goals of your school. You may even want to collaborate with another teacher so that you check each other on the process of sharing responsibility with students. Be prepared to carefully explain in what ways your program may not match the reward/punishment program your school uses. Do not give up if you become frustrated because students do not seem to be "getting it." Remember the old saw: "the more pain, the more gain." If you are making students and others uncomfortable, chances are you are stretching them, which is usually a good thing in education. Even though you need to exercise care, you may want to implement this model because in the long run it may work better for you and for your students than the one you may be using now.

The rest of this chapter explains some of the theories that provide the basis for the development of the democratic differentiated classroom model.

Theories and Practices that Support the Democratic Differentiated Classroom

To develop the democratic differentiated classroom and to understand why this model can be superior to traditional models, we explore these learning philosophies and theories that form the basis for this type of classroom:

♦ Constructivism,

♦ Learner-Centered Instruction,

♦ Backward Curriculum Design,

♦ Open-Ended (Type V) Problem Solving.

Concepts that have been proposed by educators and researchers such as Jacqueline and Martin Brooks (*The Case for Constructivist Classroom*), Robin Fogarty (*Best Practices for the Learner-Centered Classroom*), Grant Wiggins and Jay McTighe (*Understanding by Design),* and June Maker (Problem Solving Matrix in *Nurturing Giftedness in Young Children*) are explained in the following text. Additionally, I explain how I have adapted some of these ideas to accommodate the democratic differentiated classroom model.

Constructivist Classrooms

According to Brooks and Brooks (1993, p. 67), "learning is a journey, not a destination." An important aspect of constructivism comes from the work of Piaget and Inhelder (1969, 1971), who premised that "knowledge comes neither from the subject nor the object, but from the unity of the two" (Brooks & Brooks, 1993, p. 5) Brooks and Brooks draw the conclusion that good instruction empowers students to ask their own questions and find their own answers. They offer constructivism as a solution to the five unfortunate tendencies that define the classrooms in our current society. They are that teachers…

- ♦ do too much of the talking,
- ♦ rely heavily on textbooks,
- ♦ discourage cooperative learning,
- ♦ devalue student thinking, and
- ♦ believe there is a "fixed world that learners must come to know." (Brooks & Brooks, 1993, pp. 6–7)

An excellent chart that contrasts Constructivist Classrooms with Traditional classrooms follows (Brooks & Brooks, 1993, p. 17). I have added how the Constructivist Classroom supports the democratic differentiated classroom.

What Is the Democratic Differentiated Classroom?

Traditional Classroom	Constructivist Classroom	Democratic Differentiated Classroom
Teachers present ideas using part to whole and emphasize basic skills.	Teachers present ideas using whole to part. Emphasize big concepts.	Teachers collaborate with students to determine big ideas and concepts and use induction collaboratively.
Teachers stick rigidly to a fixed and prescriptive curriculum.	Teachers pursue students' questions	Teachers not only pursue students' questions, they help students learn to ask important metacognitive questions.
Teachers rely on textbooks, workbooks, and worksheets.	Teachers find primary sources of information and hands-on materials.	Teachers collaborate with students or ask students on their own to find materials.
Teachers see students as empty vessels or blank slates that they must fill.	Teachers see students as valuable thinkers whose ideas and theories are important to the overall learning process.	Teachers show students they are respected as thinkers by collaborating with them in the learning process.
Teachers provide information through lecture.	Teachers act as facilitators and mediators of learning.	Teachers facilitate the development of students as classroom leaders and planners.
Teachers focus on correct answers (convergent reasoning) to validate learning.	Teachers seek students' perspectives so that they might know how to best address misconceptions and mastery.	Teachers use students' perspectives to plan and implement curriculum decisions.
Teachers see evaluation of learning as separate from teaching.	Teachers assess student learning through a variety of authentic products.	Teachers and students collaborate to determine authentic assessment products.
Teachers assign individual work.	Students work in groups.	Students work in ways that suit them best.

Brooks and Brooks suggest that in order to change our thinking about how to teach based on constructivist theories, we need to look at the concept of paradigms. They discuss the classic work, *The Structure of Scientific Revolutions,* by Kuhn (1962), who defined the idea of a "paradigm shift" to describe what has to happen if we want to replace commonly held notions about reality. He says that we view reality through a certain perspective or lens, and that if we are willing to change the lens through which we view reality, we may be able to adjust our behaviors so that we stop doing things that are no longer effective. Implementing a democratic differentiated classroom will certainly require teachers and students to undergo a "paradigm shift" of major proportions.

Other problems that Brooks and Brooks note that are aligned with the construction of democracy and differentiation are as follows:

- ♦ Curricula are often irrelevant. For instance "When posing problems for students to study, it's crucial to avoid isolating the variables for the students, to avoid giving them more information than they need or want, and to avoid simplifying the complexity of the problem too early. Complexity often serves to generate relevance and, therefore, interest. It is oversimplification that students find confusing." (p. 39)

- ♦ Curricula is too attached to timelines and pressures to cover materials regardless of students' learning. Teachers complain that students forget so much of what has been covered. Unfortunately in many cases, it is not that they forget, it's that they never learned it, and they may never have been allowed the time to go into the kind of meaningful depth that might facilitate that learning.

- ♦ Curricula are fragmented and there is no transfer of learning from one content area to another or from one relevant concept to another. (pp. 39–42)

Brooks and Brooks admit that becoming a constructivist teacher is not easy in the present educational environment; however, it is well worth the effort. They suggest a list of 12 statements that define constructivist teachers as those who…

1. Promote and encourage student autonomy and initiative.
2. Use primary and hands-on sources.
3. Ask students to classify, analyze, predict, and create.
4. Let students make decisions about curriculum.
5. Learn students' perceptions about concepts before sharing their own.
6. Encourage active exchanges of information among students and between students and teacher.
7. Promote the open-ended inquiry process.
8. Encourage students to elaborate about their initial ideas about concepts.

9. Allow students to discover and discuss contradictions in hypotheses that they or the teacher might make about a concept.

10. Use the concept of wait-time during questioning sessions.

11. Allow time for the discovering of relationships and construction of metaphors.

12. Nurture curiosity by using the three-step learning cycle process:
    - The teacher allows the open-ended generation of ideas, hypotheses, questions (discovery phase),
    - The teacher presents information that focuses students' questions, introduces new vocabulary, and provides "concept introduction," and
    - The teacher helps students apply these new concepts to problem solving or product development. (pp. 103–118)

All of these ideas are in alignment with the democratic differentiated classroom model.

Best Practices for the Learner-Centered Classroom (Robin Fogarty)

If you want to develop a democratic differentiated classroom, you may want to consider some of the ideas from the "Learner-Centered Classroom" theorists and practitioners. Robin Fogarty provides some interesting ideas that help us look at important learning issues. She divides her areas of concern about learning into "five educational arenas: integrated curricula, thoughtful instruction, active learning, reflective transfer, and authentic assessment" (Fogarty, 1995, p. ix). These five concepts are closely aligned with the development of a democratic differentiated classroom. Here is an overview of these five concepts:

The Learner-Centered Classroom (Robin Fogarty)

Arena	Description
Integrated curricula	10 views for integrating curricula: Level 1. *Fragmented:* Each teacher takes responsibility for his content area (traditional model). Level 2. *Connected*: Connections among concepts within a content area. Level 3. *Nested*: Multiple skills addressed within the content area. <div align="center">**All above are within a discipline**</div>Level 4. *Sequenced*: Content is sequenced to coincide with another teacher's content sequence. Level 5. *Shared*: Shared planning time allows teachers in two subject areas to coordinate ideas and concepts that overlap in their content areas. Level 6. *Webbed:* Teachers use a "big idea theme" to determine what they might teach in their specific content area. Level 7. *Threaded*: Connecting metacognitive skills, such as thinking skills, through all content areas. Level 8. *Integrated*: An interdisciplinary approach that notes overlapping concepts and skills among all content areas. <div align="center">**All of the above include several disciplines**</div>Level 9. *Immersed*: The learner "filters" all content information through a common "lens" in order to see for himself how all concepts relate and fit together. Level 10. *Networked*: The learner connects with real world experts in related fields and internalizes concepts for real world problem solving. <div align="center">**All of the above exist within the learner**</div><div align="right">(p. 5)</div>

Arena	Description
Thoughtful instruction	Thoughtful instruction includes educating students for the future. Thoughtful teachers address metacognitive skills that help students learn how to make decisions, how to work with one another, and how to learn. They address what Fogarty calls the "Three Story Intellect." The first story includes *thinking skills* that might be taught by the teacher through direct instruction. The second story includes *thinking* and may include intense work from students who apply thinking skills through cooperative learning activities and by using graphic organizers. The third story includes *thoughtfulness* that requires students to apply skills to all kinds of settings and includes metacognitive reflection. (pp. 102–113)

Active learning	Many researchers have proved that cooperative learning improves student's' motivation to learn, increases academic performance, and promotes the development of skills that prepare students to work with others in the business world. But what does the best cooperative learning program look like? Fogarty and Bellanca propose the BUILD model as follows:
	   "**B**uild in higher order thinking for transfer
	     Unite teams
	     Insure individual responsibility
	     Look over and discuss the interaction
	     Develop social skills and cooperation for life" (p. 184)

Reflective transfer for lifelong learning	Fogarty has developed a framework that describes teaching for transfer as follows: "The SOMETHINGS are knowledge, concepts, skills, attitudes, principles, dispositions, and criteria. The SOMEHOW includes using strategies like *hugging*, which is setting expectations, modeling, matching, simulating, and problem-based learning. This hugging promotes spontaneous transfer and *bridging*, which anticipates applications, helps with problem solving, generalizing concepts, analyzing analogies, and metacognitive reflection. Hugging, spontaneous transfer and bridging are important if transfer of learning is to occur. The SOMEWHERE is across disciplines and into life." (pp. 253–254)
Authentic assessment	Fogarty proposes "The Tri-Assessment Model," which that includes traditional testing, portfolio, and performance. See the chart on page 16, that includes the multiple intelligences integrated with this model.

The democratic differentiated classroom (DDC) promotes these five concepts in the following ways:

1. *Integrated Curricula*: In the DDC, curriculum is organically integrated among all content areas, including the arts. Because it elevates the student's role in the learning process, it is definitely at the highest levels of integration: immersed and networked. The teacher who develops a DDC can also easily work with colleagues to extend the reach of this model beyond one classroom. From the research, we understand that at Level 1 on Fogarty's "Integrated Curriculum Continuum" (see p. 12) "Fragmented" instruction may not promote deep levels of learning for real world applications, and the DDC completely avoids this level.

2. *Thoughtful Instruction*: The DDC also addresses the concept of thoughtful instruction because it promotes the development of students' metacognitive skills through teacher prompting and guidance. It requires students to apply high levels of thoughtfulness.

3. *Active Learning*: In the DDC, students take an active role in their learning by collaboratively working in groups to solve real world problems. Students gain social skills and sometimes learn the hard way about accountability and shared responsibility.

4. *Reflective Transfer*: The DDC shifts the responsibility for learning to students, so that they begin to reflect on the importance of retaining information so that they might apply it to self-selected learning activities. The teacher facilitates this by planning activities that are the most relevant to real learning.

5. *Authentic Assessment*: The DDC asks students to show what they know and what they can do in real world applications. It extends the idea of assessment beyond best answer tests without abandoning those kinds of tests. It actually shows students how "best answer" tests can be addressed most successfully.

Understanding by Design
(Grant Wiggins and Jay McTighe)

In 1998, the Association for Supervision and Curriculum Development (ASCD) published a book by Grant Wiggins and Jay McTighe called *Understanding by Design*, also known as UbD. They propose that if teachers want to teach for "understanding," they must primarily know two things. First, they must know how to determine exactly what they want students to understand about the unit they are teaching, and second, they need to be able to recognize that their students have understood those things. In the democratic differentiated classroom model, I have added to this curriculum design model, the idea that students might participate in the decision about what they want to understand about a unit of study and how they might demonstrate they understood those things. I suggest that the teacher model for her students how to plan using this curriculum design method. Therefore, when I plan a "Democratic Differentiated" unit, I use an adaptation of the UbD model that I call "Student-Led Unit Planning." (See Chapter 3 for details). You may want to teach your students this adaptation of the UbD curriculum template as a way of helping them conceptualize an "open-ended project." This model is one of the best frameworks I've found to help teachers and students develop themes that focus on enduring understanding, skills and knowledge, acceptable evidence, and useful activities. What follows is an overview of how you might plan a UbD unit within the Democratic Differentiated Classroom model.

Step 1: One of Wiggins' and McTighe's most important ideas is that a teacher must "unpack" her standard course of study in order to determine, in language that the students can relate to, the "enduring understanding" of a unit. She should also consider how to determine, formulate, and address the essential questions that students must answer to enable student comprehension. And that this language fosters the enduring understanding, skills, and knowledge students must draw upon or develop in order to answer those essential questions. In the DDC, the teacher guides her students toward determining what they need to understand about the unit and then to choose those essential questions. You may need to provide students with some definitions, examples, and practice developing enduring understanding and essential questions. On the following page is an overview of Wiggins' and McTighe's Understanding by Design.

Understanding by Design (Grant Wiggins and Jay McTighe)

Concept	Definitions	Examples
Enduring Understanding (Some call these the "Big Ideas.") Use the template: "Students will understand that...." What comes after the "that" is the "enduring understanding statement."	Are at the heart of the discipline. Need to be uncovered. Are potentially engaging. Are enduring. We want to remember the idea for the rest of our lives. (pp. 23, 26)	Human beings are strongly connected by their feelings of love for one another. Humor is an essential element of the human spirit. Family relationships are mirrored in the norms of a culture.
Essential Questions	Go to the heart of the discipline. Recur naturally throughout one's learning and in the history of a field. Raise other important questions. Provide subject and topic-specific doorways to other essential questions. Have no one obvious "right answer." Are deliberately framed to provoke and sustain interest. (pp. 29–30)	Is love a choice? What makes people laugh? How does your relationship with your family affect your life?

Step 2: Teachers determine acceptable evidence that students have comprehended the enduring understanding and essential questions and that they have developed new knowledge and skills through focusing on those enduring understandings and essential questions.

Step 3: After determining the conceptual goals and acceptable evidence the teacher and students decide which activities they might use to make sure students learn what they want and need to learn.

The following template is a useful way to plan a unit on your own or with a team.

A UbD Template for Unit Planning

This is an example of a lesson plan for teaching teachers about UbD.

Standard: To "unpack" your standard, underline key words and phases from your standard course of study. Beginning with this phrase: "Students will understand that…." compose a sentence using the underlined words.

Enduring Understanding(s): Delete the beginning phrase, "Students will understand that…." Now you have your *Enduring Understanding* statement. For example: "The UbD framework helps teachers plan lessons that require students to understand important concepts determined by their standard course of study."

Essential Questions (four to six are sufficient): With all the concepts teachers are required to cover and the limited time they have to teach them, how do they determine which of these concepts to focus on? What skills do teachers need to develop to help them learn the concepts of UbD? What kinds of assessment(s) will provide the best measure of teachers' achievement related to the study of UbD? What activities and materials will engage teachers so that they will be motivated to learn the enduring understanding(s) for this unit?

Knowledge	Skills
Six facets of understanding. What are enduring understandings and essential questions?	Reading comprehension. Collaboration skills. Writing ability.

Acceptable Evidence: Teachers fill out the template with an appropriate lesson plan and they present a video-taped lesson from the UbD lesson plan.

Activities: Teachers read the book *Understanding by Design* by Grant Wiggins and Jay McTighe. Teachers participate in a discussion group during which they go over one chapter of the book at a time and apply the strategies to their own classrooms.

Evaluation/Reflection (How did the unit go?): Reflect with other teachers about how well the lesson went. Consider developing a rubric to determine how well you did.

Open-Ended Projects

One more concept you need to understand before planning a democratic differentiated classroom is the idea of "Open-ended Projects," which comes in part from my interpretation of June Maker's (1996) continuum of problem types as follows:

Part of Problem	Type I	Type II	Type III	Type IV	Type V
Problem	Clearly defined	Clearly defined	Clearly defined	Clearly defined	Find the problem, fuzzy, ill defined
Solution	Right Answers	Best Answers	Answers vary	Answers vary	Answers vary
Method	Clearly determined	Range of methods	Range of methods	Discover a method	Discover a method

In the democratic differentiated classroom, I use mostly "Type V" problems for students' projects. I ask students to "discover a method" for answering one or more of the essential questions determined by our unit. Students have to "find the problem," which is ill defined and fuzzy as they begin their inquiry based on an essential question or questions they have chosen to answer. I ask students to complete a "Project Proposal" form (see Chapter 4) to explain how they will determine answers to their essential questions. I meet with each student or student group to go over this form and to guide students toward making good learning choices. One way to tie these projects more closely to content is to require that the project be based on a certain text or texts chosen by the teacher or the students. It is also a good idea to ask students to cite their sources even if they are not writing a paper about their subject.

Summary

The Differentiated Democratic Classroom is identified by collaboration among teachers and students. One reason for labeling it differentiated is that instruction is fair to all learners. It is democratic because students get to make choices by voting on critical aspects of the curriculum. As with any democracy, students and teachers cannot do whatever they please. Rules and guidelines must be established and respected within the classroom and the whole school. As the adult in the classroom, the teacher has more expertise regarding important classroom decisions; however, she uses respectful explanation and reminding to convince students to agree with her rather than making demands for compliance. The truly respectful teacher will understand and respect students' perspectives and find ways to guide them. Most students do understand and support the idea that school is a place to learn and most can be convinced that even if the learning is not always fun, it is important. The differentiated democratic classroom seeks fairness and motivation and assumes that by offering these two important constructs, discipline and learning will follow seamlessly.

This book explains how to teach students using this model by answering these essential questions:

  ♦ How do teacher and student know if students have learned in the democratic differentiated classroom?
  ♦ How do we involve students in their own learning for democracy?
  ♦ How do we group students for differentiation?
  ♦ What tools (strategies) are organic to democracy and differentiation?
  ♦ How to develop a democratic differentiated unit?

In closing, John Dewey (1916) said "A society which makes provision for participation in its good of all its members on equal terms and which secures flexible readjustment of its institutions through interaction of different forms of associated life is in so far democratic. Such a society must have a type of education, which gives individuals a personal interest in social relationships and control, and the habits of mind which secure social change without introducing disorder (p. 99)." In terms of the preservation of our democratic nation, we must use educational practices that develop citizens who think for themselves and who do not need to be told by a dictator how to think or act. Our educational system must encourage and allow students to make choices, and we must differentiate instruction so that we will prepare our children and young people to preserve democracy.

2

How Do Teachers *and* Students Know if Students Have Learned in the Democratic Differentiated Classroom?

**Touchstone Tasks
(Wiggins and McTighe)**

Evaluation of Student Learning

Rubrics

Summary

If you plan to implement a democratic differentiated classroom, one of the most important steps to take is to determine strategies that will help you and your students know if students have learned in this special environment. First we need to get some terms straight. How do learning, assessment, and evaluation fit together?

- *Learning* is what happens when students gain knowledge, skills, and attitudes.

- *Assessment* is what happens when teachers ask students what they know, what they can do, and how they feel, or what they believe about what they are learning. (Trussell-Cullen, 1998, p. 7)

  Assessment is also what happens when students ask themselves and each other what they know, what they can do, and how they feel or what they believe about what they are learning.

- *Evaluation* is what happens when teachers determine acceptable evidence of learning, what that evidence means, and what to do about it. [Students might be added here too, as peer evaluators and self-evaluators.] (Trussell-Cullen, 1998, p. 7)

Assessing student achievement is a large issue and one that has been researched and debated since students and teachers have existed. In 2001, the Committee on the Foundations of Assessment published their findings in a book titled, *Knowing What Students Know: The Science and Design of Educational Assessment* (Pellegrino, Chudowsky, Glaser, 2001). For three years this committee met to consider new information about research and practice in the area of educational assessment. I will summarize some of their key findings that relate to us in the democratic differentiated classroom.

Knowing What Students Know

Categories	Description
Guiding principles	"(1) something important should be learned from every assessment situation, and (2) the information gained should ultimately help improve learning." (pp. 7–8)
Differing purposes	Classroom assessment is powerful if it is based on the teacher's knowledge of her students' learning histories. Large-scale standardized tests have limited usefulness in a teacher's classroom because their purpose is to gather information that is relevant across time and place. "… the contrast between classroom and large-scale assessment arises from the different purposes they serve and contexts in which they are used." (p. 8) The primary purpose for large-scale standardized tests can be for program analysis, not "to produce reliable individual student scores…" (p. 9)
Connecting instruction with assessment	"In the classroom, providing students with information about particular qualities of their work and about what they can do to improve is crucial for maximizing learning." (p. 8)
Putting theory into practice	Because findings from cognitive research on student learning are not always easy to put into practice, "Teachers need theoretical training, as well as practical training and assessment tools, to be able to implement formative assessment effectively in their classrooms." (p. 8)
Benefits of large-scale standard- ized tests	Large-scale standardized tests can be of help if they are designed and used appropriately. They can define "academic competence societies consider worthy of recognition and reward." (p. 8)
Teaching to the test	Teaching to specific items on a large-scale test is not desirable; however, teaching to the theory of learning that is reflected in the test can provide a "positive direction for instruction." (p. 8)
Benefits for students	"For classroom or large-scale assessment to be effective, students must understand and share the goals for learning. Students learn more when they understand (and even participate in developing) the criteria by which their work will be evaluated, and when they engage in peer and self-assessment during which they apply those criteria. These practices develop students' metacognitive abilities, which …are necessary for effective learning." (p. 9)

Shifting emphasis and funding to classroom assessment	The current assessment environment values large-scale assessment over classroom assessment. Large amounts of money are spent on these large-scale assessments. "More of the research, development, and training investment must be shifted toward the classroom where teaching and learning occur." (p. 9)
The vision	"A vision for the future is that assessments at all levels, from classroom to state, will work together in a system that is comprehensive, coherent, and continuous. Assessment at all levels would be linked back to the same underlying model of student learning and would provide indications of student growth over time." (p. 9)

If you want to successfully implement the democratic differentiated classroom, you will want to have an understanding of the misconceptions about learning, assessment, and evaluation. In his book, *Assessment: In the Learner-Centered Classroom,* Alan Trussell-Cullen explains several misconceptions as follows (1998, pp. 9-18). (Note how often he mentions the importance of student involvement in assessment):

Assessment in the Learner-Cenered Classroom (Alan Trussell-Cullen)

Misconceptions	Reality
1. Assessment is something teachers do after learning or to interrupt learning.	In good teaching assessment is going on all the time. Assessment is infused in a planning, teaching, learning, assessing spiral that is on-going and organic to the entire learning process.
2. Assessment is something only teachers do.	Students need to learn how to assess their own learning, and teachers should hand over some of the power of evaluation to students for two reasons: (1) it makes students more independent as learners, and (2) it helps teachers survive the mounds of paper work that go with being the "chief judge" of student work.
3. Assessment is done to the learner.	In line with the misconception above, good assessment is something learners do for themselves. Good teachers can model for students how they assess their own teaching.
4. Assessment involves measurement-like numbers and grades.	Number and letter grades are one dimensional, but learning is multifaceted; therefore, there is not a good match between learning and measurement with numbers and grades.
5. We think of learning as linear because of the historical models Henry Ford (assembly line) and B. F. Skinner (stimulus-response).	Learning is not a simple cause and effect or stimulus-response process. It is varied and at times unpredictable. Linear models for assessing learning do not take into consideration the many differences in students.
6. We think about learning like we think about sports and business where competition is the organizing factor.	Thinking about learning in terms of competition, i.e., winning and losing, is dangerous. Learning should not be thought of in these terms. It is varied and multifaceted and cannot be thought of in simple terms.

7. Assessment is something you do by testing. This is a BIG misconception.	What is a test anyway? It is a simulation of a behavior you want to measure. There are four good questions we should answer before we use a test to assess learning: How valid is the test? (How close to real is the simulation of the behavior we want to measure?) How reliable is the test? (Is this a typical response for this student?) How useful is the test to the learner and the teacher? (Is the test going to make instruction more effective? Will it enhance learning?) How necessary is the test? (Why use an artificial simulation when we can use authentic assessment procedures?)
8. Assessment requires us to classify or label children.	Classifications and labels focus on what a child cannot do and these labels stick.
9. There is a right way to assess, and when we discover it, we will require all teachers to do it this way and never talk about it again.	Although it is important to be systematic and consistent with assessment, each learning environment is unique and has its own set of issues that a "one-way" solution would not address.

Many of these myths assure us that allowing students to choose how they will be assessed and how they should be evaluated is the best direction. In the democratic differentiated classroom, we encourage students to decide how they will address curriculum themes and goals. With the teacher's guidance, students plan their own assessments. Chapter 3 provides suggestions for helping students collaborate with the teacher to determine how their work will be assessed.

If you plan to implement a democratic differentiated classroom, you don't have to let students plan everything because they can learn a great deal from you in terms of assessment. It is a good idea to show them some types of assessments about which they may not be aware. Here is an overview of Trussell-Cullen's "The Learning Assessment Toolbox" (1998, p. 51). I have included what I consider a well-known strategy first, and then a less well-known strategy. I suggest you read his book for many more creative and useful strategies.

The Learning Assessment Toolbox (An Overview)

Well-Known Strategy					
Observation	Interaction	Re-creation	Reflection	Simulation	Artifact Collection
Anecdotal notebook (p. 55): Record observations of each child's learning progress. Share how you assess the work with the child.	Questioning (p. 65) Use a variety of question types: Closed, open-ended, probing, and a variety of responses: Nonjudge-mental, redirected, rephrased.	Role play (p. 79): Students act out scenes or concepts. They might also conduct "in role" interviews or talk shows with important characters from a story or event.	Personal journal (p. 88): Students write about what they learned in school today: their thoughts and feelings, and whatever else they want to write.	Tests (pp. 95–96): These can be standard-ized or teacher made. The problem with these tests is not the tests themselves, but how they might be used.	Learner-managed learning portfolio (p. 100): Students set learning goals for themselves and collect evidence of attaining those goals.
Well-Known Strategy					
Camera in the class (p. 59): Take pictures of students' progress. Post pictures on a board.	Our class experts (p. 71): Teacher provides an "Experts List." Students write what they do well beside their name on the list.	Moving learning around the language bases (p. 75): A way for students to show what they know about a topic; they can move around the language bases (oral, written, visual, body) as they explain what they know.	"How I feel about" checklist (p. 94) from E. de Bono: Students react to an event by commenting on a "plus," a "minus," and an "interest-ing."	Testing in pairs (p. 99): Students work with a buddy to test each other. You might give them a chart to record the results of their tests with each other.	Mini time capsules (p. 104): At the beginning of the year collect samples of students' work and interesting information about them. Bury the information in a capsule. At the end of the year open it up and see how things have changed.

Touchstone Tasks (Wiggins and McTighe)

There are numerous methods for assessing learning; however, some may be more substantial in terms of determining real learning. You may want to share the idea of "touchstone tasks" (Wiggins and McTighe, 1998) with your students. Here is a quote from their book *Understanding by Design* that captures the idea of these important tasks.

> "We as educators should identify at the local and national levels *touchstone tasks:* the most important performances that can fruitfully be used over time to assess enduring understandings and core processes, or abilities such as effective writing, research, problem solving, and oral communication.
>
> Using these reiterative (repetitive) tasks provides educators, parents, and students with rich and credible evidence that key understandings and proficiencies are being developed over time." (p. 86)

Also from Wiggins and McTighe is an interesting chart to help you distinguish between thinking as an "Assessor" and thinking as an "Activity Designer" (p. 68).

Two Different Approaches to Assessment

Thinking like an Assessor	Thinking like an Activity Designer
What would be acceptable evidence of understanding?	What activities would be interesting and engaging as we learn about this topic?
What types of performance tasks will "anchor the unit and focus" the students' work?	What resources and materials do I have and need to get to teach this topic?
How can I tell who is really learning this versus who seems to be learning it?	What assignments will I give: homework and classwork?
What criteria will I use to judge students' work?	How will I grade students and justify those grades to their parents?
What misunderstandings might students have and how can I check for them?	Did the activities work?

It is important to share these ideas with students so that they can share your concern for their learning. You may need to teach students about how to plan for learning.

Every teacher should have a toolkit filled with assessment strategies she shares with her students. Here is a list of some of the best:

My Favorite Assessment Tools

Multiple Intelligences projects that ask students to use their strengths to demonstrate mastery or understanding of a concept of set of concepts.

Personal Journals or *Learning Logs* that ask students to reflect about what they have learned.

Any kind of *skit* or *dramatization;* live, on film, with actors, or with puppets.

Games and *simulations* that require students to demonstrate knowledge or skills.

The big *essay* question or *short answer* paragraph.

Tricky multiple choice questions that require students to use higher-level thinking skills and in which every answer is possible, but only one is *best*. This kind of test aligns with important standardized tests such as the SAT and ACD.

The *five-question quiz* that acts as review or to introduce a new topic.

The *Socratic seminar,* which is a great measure of oral skills and thinking.

Technology presentations such as PowerPoint or short film documentaries.

A *research paper* or *project* of any kind.

A *portfolio* of students' work.

I provide explanations and examples of each of these strategies in my book, *Handbook on Differentiated Instruction for Middle and High School* (Northey, 2005).

Evaluation of Student Learning

The above list falls into the area of assessment, but what about evaluation? At what point do we (teachers and students) decide what is acceptable evidence and what we will do with that evidence? Determining acceptable evidence that students have learned is a serious consideration and we should take care to know when and why we are assessing what students know, what they can do, and what their attitudes are about their learning. Trussell-Cullen (1998) offers an excellent idea to help us decide some important questions about assessment. He proposes an "Assessment Audit" that may help us develop a realistic perspective about the purpose(s) of our assessments or evaluations of our students' achievement in our classes.

Assessment Audit

Who Is the Test for?	What do They Need the Information for?	What Kind of Information do They Need?
Teachers should have a clear idea of which stakeholders will be interested in the results of the test. For most teachers stakeholders include: students, parents, principals, district officials, and policy makers. The teacher is also included in this list.	This is an important question because different stakeholders may want tests for varying reasons.	Once we have the answers to the first two questions, we can begin to determine the kinds of assessments to use and how we might organize and explain the results for the benefit of our students.

Trussell-Cullen leaves students out of his audit, but (where appropriate) you may want to include them as much as possible.

Most teachers have had lots of experience administering all kinds of tests to evaluate students' learning, but one of the most useful measures of students' learning is not a test, but a rubric.

Rubrics

What exactly is a rubric? According to *RubiStar,* a rubric is a scoring tool that allows evaluators to determine levels of performance on the important aspects of a piece of work. One of the most important aspects of a rubric is that it allows those doing that piece of work to have a good idea of how the evaluator will determine its quality. Evaluators usually give scores between 1 and 4, and then they add up those scores to determine the total. Some rubrics designate the level of help the teacher might provide. The most valuable aspect of a rubric is that it helps teachers and students define the "quality" of the work.

There are two basic kinds of rubrics analytical and holistic. Analytical rubrics break the description of the levels of performance into discrete parts while holistic rubrics list the parts as one whole statement or paragraph. One might use an analytical rubric for formative evaluation and a holistic rubric for summative evaluation. What follows are examples of the two kinds of rubrics.

Here is a rubric I designed with the help of RubiStar.

Analytical Rubric: "Making a Brochure"

Category	1	2	3	4	Score
Writing Organization	Less than half of the sections of the brochure have a clear beginning, middle, and end.	Most sections of the brochure have a clear beginning, middle, and end.	Almost all sections of the brochure have a clear beginning, middle, and end.	Each section in the brochure has a clear beginning, middle, and end.	
Attractiveness & Organization	The brochure's formatting and organization of material are confusing to the reader.	The brochure has well-organized information.	The brochure has attractive formatting and well-organized information.	The brochure has exceptionally attractive formatting and well-organized information	
Content & Accuracy	Fewer than 80% of the facts in the brochure are accurate.	80–89% of the facts in the brochure are accurate.	90–99% of the facts in the brochure are accurate.	All facts in the brochure are accurate.	
Graphics/ Pictures	Graphics do not go with the accompanying text or appear to be chosen randomly.	Graphics go well with the text, but there are too few and the brochure seems "text heavy" or there are too many and they distract from the text.	Graphics go well with the text, but none of them are original or interesting use of copied ones.	Graphics are original or interesting use of copied graphics. They go well with the text and there is a good mix of graphics and text.	
				Total Score:	

Holistic Rubric for the Same Brochure: "Making a Brochure"

1	2	3	4
Less than one half of the sections of the brochure have a clear beginning, middle, and end. The brochure's formatting and organization of material are confusing to the reader. Fewer than 80% of the facts in the brochure are accurate. Graphics do not go with the accompanying text or appear to be randomly chosen.	Most sections of the brochure have a clear beginning, middle, and end. The brochure has well-organized information. 80–89% of the facts in the brochure are accurate. Graphics go well with the text, but there are too few and the brochure seems text heavy or there are too many and they distract from the text.	Almost all sections of the brochure have a clear beginning, middle, and end. The brochure has attractive formatting and well-organized information. 90–99% of the facts in the brochure are accurate. Graphics go well with the text, but none of them are original.	Each section in the brochure has a clear beginning, middle, and end. The brochure has exceptionally attractive formatting and well-organized information. All facts in the brochure are accurate. Graphics are original or interesting use of copied graphics. They go well with the text and there is a good mix of graphics and text.

Level: _____

One of the challenges with using rubrics is converting the scores to grades. Here is how I do it. For an analytical rubric…

Give each category a point value. For instance, in the above rubric, each category could be worth 25 points, or you could weight the points in some way, such as 20 points for writing, 20 points for organization, 50 points for accuracy, and 10 points for graphics. Deduct points for each category based on the student's attainment of the rubric standards. For example: Jane's brochure has the following features:

◆ For **Writing and Organization**—each section has a clear beginning, middle and end. Score 25 points.

◆ For **Attractiveness and Organization**—the brochure has attractive formatting, but it is not exceptional. One portion is somewhat sloppy. Deduct 5 points. Score 20.

◆ For **Content and Accuracy**—the student has made one error in accuracy. Deduct 1 point. Score 24.

◆ For **Graphics/Pictures**—there are too many graphics and not enough text; however, the graphics do go with the text and there is one original graphic. Deduct 11 points. Score 14.

Scores are:

Writing and Organization	25
Attractiveness and Organization	20
Content and Accuracy	24
Graphics/Pictures	15
Total Score	84 = C+

The Holistic Rubric scoring process:

4	=	no loss of points	=	A+
3	=	loss of 1–11 points	=	89–99 = A, A–, or B+
2	=	loss of 12–23 points	=	88–77 = B, C+, or C
1	=	lose of 24 or more points	=	76–0 = D+, D, D– or F

Or you can say that Level 4 = A (well-above average), Level 3 = B (above average), Level 2 = C (average), Level 1 = D (below average) and not doing the work at all is an F. Some systems consider a score of 2 to be failing (below average) and 1 to be well-below average. Also in some lower grades, it is a good policy not to give zeroes.

Designing rubrics has become quite easy with all the online resources available to teachers to help them construct rubrics. You might also encourage students to explore these rubric-making sites. Here is an annotated list of the top four I found online by using Google.com.

Rubric-Making Web Sites

Website and Address	Description
RubiStar http://Rubistar.4teachers.org	A free tool to help teachers create excellent rubrics. Easy to use and comprehensive.
TeAchnology: The Web Portal for Educators http://www.teachnology.com/	Has free rubric maker capacity for a wide variety of topics from behavior modification to evaluating oral projects.
Kathy Schrock's Guide for Educators http://schooldiscovery.com/ schrockguide/assess.html.	Has excellent subject-specific and general rubrics and web-based rubrics that include assessing WebQuests, school web pages, classroom web pages, and student web pages.
Midlink Magazine Teacher Tools http://www.ncsu.edu/midlink/ ho.html	Has a wide variety of multimedia rubrics, software evaluation rubrics and many more.

All of the information shared with you here might also be shared with the students to help them truly become your partners in the process of assessing and evaluating their learning. See Chapter 3 for an explanation of the "Student-Led Unit Planning" process. In that chapter I have included how to develop the student-led assessment process, which includes developing a "Consensus Rubric."

Open-ended projects fit well in the democratic differentiated classroom; however, you also need to teach students how to respond to our current reality, the multiple-choice test.

Constructing Multiple Choice Tests

Standardized tests are a current reality and they have almost always functioned as the primary gateway into colleges and universities; therefore, teachers must not ignore the importance of teaching their students the strategy of identifying best answers in multiple-choice tests (i.e., convergent reasoning). Teachers often have access to multiple choice test formats provided for them by their districts or provided in test-preparation workbooks; however, teachers can greatly increase their capability for providing multiple-choice question answering practice for their students by doing two things.

- ♦ Learning to write high-level multiple-choice questions based on textbooks and other print and nonprint resources.
- ♦ Teaching students to write high-level multiple-choice questions themselves. I will explain how to teach students to write multiple-choice questions in Chapter 3 a section called "Student-Led Questioning."

Some researchers say that students think *more* when they ask questions than when they answer them.

Writing Your Own Tests

These are some steps that might help you write your own multiple-choice questions.

1. Analyze the types of question stems your students will be asked to respond to on standardized multiple-choice tests. Make a list of these stems if your system does not provide them for you.

2. As you read and go over the materials you have for your content area, use those stems to construct questions that address the most important aspects of your materials.

3. Choose answers that for the most part *could* be true, but only one answer is *best*. This step can be tricky because your questions need to be fair. Avoid questions that are based on opinion or that might reflect a bias and focus on those that reflect the *best* interpretation or analysis. Make sure you do not include more than one *correct* answer.

4. Find a quick way to score these multiple-choice tests. The "Bubble Sheet" is a quick and easy way for students to respond to multiple-choice tests, it is aligned with the standardized tests, and you can easily hand score it if you do not have access to a scoring machine. If your school does not have "Bubble Sheets" or a scoring machine, here is how to make your own "Bubble Sheets" and how to score your students multiple-choice responses:

Making and Hand Scoring a Multiple Choice Test Bubble Sheet

Step 1: Make the test.

Step 2: Print enough copies of a "bubble sheet" for all class members and one for the key. You might use *Catpin.com* or other websites that help you construct bubble sheets.

Step 3: Take the test yourself (this will help you discover any mistakes you have made) to make the key.

Step 4: Laminate the key.

Step 5: If you do not have a hole puncher with a long neck, make slits down each row.

Step 6: Use a hole-puncher to punch out the correct answers on your key.

Step 7: Use a colored marker to mark students' incorrect answers on their tests through the holes in your key.

You can quickly see how many they missed to determine their score.

Summary

In the democratic differentiated classroom, teachers share the responsibility of assessment and evaluation with their students. They ask students to use peer evaluation, student-made tests, and self-evaluation to make sure learning is taking place. Every assignment includes clear standards for excellence that students understand and may even help create. It is critical that teachers constantly assess and evaluate learning especially if they are venturing from the traditional classroom.

3

Involving Students in Their Own Learning

Student-Led Unit Planning

Student-Led Conferences

Robin Fogarty's THEMES

H. Lynn Erickson's Concept-Based Curriculum Ideas

Summary

The National Research Council (NRC) reported that students come to the classroom with preconceptions about how the world works. If their initial understanding is not engaged, they may fail to grasp the new concepts and information that are taught, or they may learn them for purposes of a test but revert to their preconceptions outside the classroom. The council also states that teachers should address students' metacognitive processes so that they might take control of their own learning by defining learning goals and monitoring their progress toward achieving those goals. (pp. 10–13) The ideas from the NRC fit perfectly with the goals of the democratic differentiated classroom. Three critical strategies support his model.

 ♦ Student-Led Unit Planning
 ♦ Student-Led Conferences
 ♦ Student-Led Questioning

Student-Led Unit Planning and Student-Led Questioning are my own innovations; however, the student-led conference idea has been used in schools for several years. This chapter presents my adaptation of the process.

Student-Led Unit Planning

This is a step-by-step guide to involving students in their learning.

Step 1: Make a list of the *themes* that over-arch concepts you teach within your grade level or content area. Give the list to your students and ask them to keep the list in their notebooks for the entire year. Tell students they also may add to the list.

Here is a list of possible themes:

Some Theme/Topic Choices

Family	Civil Rights	Depression	Oppression
Holocaust	Renaissance/Rebirth	Immigration	Civil War
War	Justice	Survival	Relationships
Diversity	Power	Transformation	Humor
Freedom	Change	Balance	Love
Heroes	Friendship	Growing up	Tragedy
Courage	The Fantastic	Choices	Integrity
Home	Heritage	Tools	Connections
Geometry	Expectations	Patterns	Observation
Water	Music	Systems	

Step 2: Have a meeting with the class to determine which theme should guide the formation of the unit of study. Use this process:

1. Teacher asks students to suggest a theme and explain why they want that theme.
2. Teacher writes the theme on the board and asks if any other students want to speak on behalf of that theme or against that theme.
3. Every student has a chance to suggest a theme.
4. After all themes are on the board, students vote on their favorites and the majority wins.

     Note: Sometimes you may have a close vote, and students may want a revote between the top two or three vote-getters.

Integrating with other teachers: If you want to integrate the choosing of themes with other teachers, rotating the decision about the theme among the teachers who are integrating their instruction may prove helpful. For instance, if a team of teachers has decided to integrate their instruction, students may choose the first theme in a science class, the second theme in a Language Arts or English class, the third theme in a Social Studies or History class and so forth.

Step 3: KWL: As soon as possible do a KWL lesson around the theme that won.

*   What students already **K**now about the theme
*   What they **W**ant to learn about the theme, and
*   How they want to **L**earn about the theme)

Proceed in this manner:

1. Ask students what they know about the theme first. This helps you have some idea about their "preconceptions" about the topic and gives you some ideas about the direction to take when you plan the unit.
2. Next find out what students want to learn about the topic. Write this "want to learn" in the form of *generalizations* (similarly known as: *enduring understandings, essential understandings, big ideas*). Help students determine this concept-based statement or statements ("Students will understand that…") that will be the focus of your unit of study. If you believe that developing generalizations is too hard for your students, show them *your* generalizations for their approval. Next lead them through asking essential questions that are over-arching, meaningful, and aligned with your discipline. Also give them examples of the skills and knowledge they will use and/or learn as they explore this theme. Most importantly give them ideas for acceptable evidence (product ideas) that they have learned about his theme and share ideas for activities that will help them prepare their product. Note: In order to do this step, you should have a clear understanding of the process of unit planning through the development of generalizations and essential questions.

3. Ask students how they want to learn about the theme. Most often, students will want to do a creative project they choose. Also, they will most likely want to learn with a partner or in a small group.

Step 4: The best way to allow students to determine how they learn about the theme is by offering open-ended theme-based project choices. Ask students to think about how they might answer one or more of the essential questions we have determined as important. Then ask them to fill out a "Project Proposal" form that they will submit to you. Below is an example of a Project Proposal form to use in assigning an open-ended theme-based project for any unit of study. Students fill out this form with the teacher's assistance and then take a certain amount of time to prepare their projects.

Deadlines: The time limits may be determined through collaboration with the teacher. If students help establish deadlines, you will have less complaining when the deadlines occur. You might also allow students to extend a deadline by class vote if you know they have worked hard, but may truly need more time. This flexibility with deadlines can be abused, but if students truly need more time, you will see a much better turn-in rate if you are flexible. You might also allow students to get notes from parents that can extend a deadline. If you believe you are working in collaboration with parents, you need to trust their judgment concerning their child's capacity to respond to a deadline. Here is an example of a handout I give my students to help them determine how they will learn about a theme:

Project Proposal

You have two weeks to complete this project.

Please answer the following questions about your project and return this form to me during our conference:

1. Who is involved in this project?

2. What is your theme?

3. What is your "big idea"? ["We will learn that…" (finish this thought as a complete sentence)]

4. List one or more essential questions your project will answer.

5. List skills you will use and/or learn in order to complete this project.

6. List knowledge you will use or gain in order to complete this project.

7. Explain how you will present acceptable evidence that you have addressed your big idea and answered your questions.

8. Provide a detailed list of things you will do to complete your project.

Step 5: Briefly meet with each person or group to go over the form and to make sure they are heading in a good direction. Here are some guidelines:

 ♦ Ask them questions that get them to focus on attainable learning goals.

 ♦ Do not let them get too ambitious, too narrow, or shallow.

 ♦ Help them choose measurable objectives within their chosen theme.

 ♦ Make sure they understand what kinds of data they might need to gather in order to answer their essential questions.

 ♦ Make sure they have the equipment and capability of completing the products they would like to produce. For instance, some students may want to make a movie, but have no camera or film editing capabilities.

 ♦ Help them learn to discuss metacognitive skills (talking about their learning) so that they know to write about the "skills" and "knowledge" they will gain as they investigate their chosen theme.

 ♦ Give struggling students lots of examples and help if you want them to successfully fill out this form.

 ♦ Do not let them set themselves up to fail.

 ♦ *Helpful hint:* Discuss the project with them as you would discuss planning a lesson with a colleague. This is a true collaboration that will help students share the responsibility for their own learning.

If you allow students to take this kind of responsibility for their learning, you may need to provide some suggestions or some accountability structure. Here are some useful handouts and forms:

Kinesthetic (Hands-On) Activity Ideas

Hint: Make sure your choice of activity goes well with the theme or essential question(s) you are answering.

Dramatizing	Games
Skit	Jeopardy
Pantomime	Board games
Tableau (a scene frozen in time to show an idea or theme—like a live picture)	Charades
Puppet show—paper or cardboard stick puppets, cloth puppets, sock puppets, felt puppets, shadow puppets	Pictionary
Enactment	Capture the flag
Demonstration	Who Wants to Be a Millionaire
Cheer	Survivor

Dramatizing	Games
Using hand and/or body motions to act out a song, a poem, or any piece of information	The Newly-Weds
Students assume the persona of a concept and act it out (i.e., students become a cell body, students become a math line, students become a primary document)	The Dating Game
Talk show (TV or radio), news show, or comedy show	The Gong Show
Weather show	
Documentary	
Short film	

Experiments

Science lab

Action survey (i.e., ask questions and students move to the locations that represent their answers)

Putting something together or creating something as a team or as an individual

Building something and checking its quality through competition with other builders

Activities that demonstrate group dynamics

Accountability and Time Frame

If you are concerned that students will not work steadily on an open-ended project, you can require them to fill out a sheet like the Project Time Sheet. The best time frame should be adjusted based on the students' grade level. Younger students need more check points so that you might check their progress daily to weekly. Some teachers give year-long projects for secondary students, but check progress at set points along the way. For middle school students, you may want to assign projects that can be constructed in two weeks to a month.

Project Time Sheet

Name:_____ Project Title:_____

Project Due Date:_____

Please record the date, activity, start time and end time for each time you work on your project. Ask your parent, guardian, or teacher to verify each date, activity, and time you worked on your project. Turn this completed form in with your project.

Date	Activity	Start	End	Signature

Step 6: Hold a classroom meeting during which you and students determine the standards for the project. After students have had time to begin working on these projects, they will be better prepared to fill out the Consensus Rubric. Give students a blank rubric and work together as a whole class to decide what each level looks like as it is applied to the projects they are preparing. Ask students to fill in the rubric as you decide the categories and levels of achievement for each of those categories. This is an exciting process because students generally have high standards for their work. Try to get at least three good descriptive phrases for each level under each category. Key questions to use as you are guiding students through this process are:

♦ What categories should be used to evaluate our projects?

♦ Does _____ (a suggested category) fit under another category or can it stand alone?

   Some typical categories might be: organization, originality, content, creativity, and/or technical quality.

♦ What does a 4 look like? (And on down to a 1).

♦ What point value does each level get?
   (For 4 categories, I suggest: 4 = 25, 3 = 20, 2 = 15, and 1 = 10.)

Rubric

Propose a rubric for your project:

Category	Level 1	Level 2	Level 3	Level 4

4 = student receives all points (A+), 3 = loss of 1–15 points (A to B-), 2 = loss of 16–30 (C+ to D-) points, and 1 = loss of all 31 points (F)

Step 7: A few days before the project is due, have students sign up to present their projects (see the sign up sheet that follows). On the sign-up sheet include who is presenting, what they are presenting, what equipment they might need, and how much time they need. This sheet helps determine how much class time is needed and what needs to be set up to make sure the project presentations flow smoothly.

Presentation Sign-Up Sheet

Please sign up with your group.

Names of Group Members Presenting	Title of Presentation	Materials Needed	Amount of Time Needed

Balance: A Word of Caution

Letting students choose the themes they want to learn and how they want to learn about them is highly motivational and exciting. Students take ownership of the learning process and its content and become stronger and more capable for having done so; however, this freedom must be balanced with teacher decision making. As their teacher, make sure students have access to certain aspects of the curriculum that may be out of their frame of reference or that they might not know is important based on their limited experiences. Balance their choices with concepts and skills you know they need to develop and leverage some of those less thrilling skills and concepts in exchange for the more creative and self-selected activities. By allowing students choices, you are better able to respectfully require them to stretch toward less interesting and more difficult tasks that are necessary for their growth. Tell your students that school assignments are like reading a book. Some books you choose and you read them for pleasure or because you are interested in them. Other books you read because they are part of your job or you need to know the information in them to prepare you to do something you have hopefully chosen. Students are more likely to stretch intellectually and physically if they know their choices are valued and that you are on their side when it comes to learning.

Example of a Student-Led Unit

Standards

1.02 Explore expressive materials that are read, heard, and/or viewed by:
- monitoring comprehension for understanding of what is read, heard, and/or viewed.
- analyzing the characteristics of expressive works.
- determining the effect of literary devices and/or strategies on the reader/viewer/listener.
- making connections between works, self, and related topics.
- comparing and/or contrasting information.
- drawing inferences and/or conclusions.
- determining the main idea and/or significance of events.
- creating an artistic interpretation that connects self to the work.
- discussing print and nonprint expressive works formally and informally.

1.03 Interact appropriately in group settings by:
- listening attentively.
- showing empathy.
- contributing relevant comments connecting personal experiences to content.
- monitoring own understanding of the discussion and seeking clarification as needed.

5.01 Increase fluency, comprehension, and insight through a meaningful and comprehensive literacy program by:
- using effective reading strategies to match type of text.
- reading self-selected literature and other materials of individual interest.
- reading literature and other materials selected by the teacher.
- interpreting text by explaining elements such as plot, theme, point of view, characterization, mood, and style.
- recognizing underlying messages in order to identify theme(s) within and across works.
- extending understanding by creating products for different purposes, different audiences, and within various contexts.
- exploring relationships between and among characters, ideas, concepts and/or experiences.

6.01 Demonstrate an understanding of conventional written and spoken expression by:

- using a variety of sentence types correctly, punctuating them properly, and avoiding fragments and run-ons.
- using appropriate subject-verb agreement and verb tense that are appropriate for the meaning of the sentence.
- demonstrating the different roles of the parts of speech in sentence construction.
- using pronouns correctly, including clear antecedents and correct case.
- using phrases and clauses correctly (e.g., prepositional phrases, appositives, dependent and independent clauses).
- determining the meaning of unfamiliar vocabulary words by using context clues, a dictionary, a glossary, a thesaurus, and/or structural analysis (roots, prefixes, suffixes) of words.
- extending vocabulary knowledge by learning and using new words.
- exploring the role and use of dialects and of standard English to appreciate appropriate usage in different contexts.
- developing an awareness of language conventions and usage during oral presentations.

6.02 Identify and edit errors in spoken and written English by:

- reviewing and using common spelling rules, applying common spelling patterns, and developing and mastering an individualized list of words that are commonly misspelled.
- applying proofreading symbols when editing.
- producing final drafts that demonstrate accurate spelling and the correct use of punctuation and capitalization.
- developing an awareness of errors in everyday speech.

3.02 Explore the problem solution process by:

- preparing individual and/or group essays and presentations that focus on the diagnosis of a problem and possible solutions.

2.02 Use multiple sources of print and nonprint information in designing and developing informational materials (such as brochures, newsletters, and infomercials) through:

- exploring a variety of sources from which information may be attained (e.g., books, Internet, electronic databases, CD-ROM).
- distinguishing between primary and secondary sources.
- analyzing the effects of the presentation and/or the accuracy of information.

From "NC Standard Course of Study" http://www.ncpublicschools.org/curriculum/languagearts/scos/1004/23grade6.

Enduring Understanding: Music inspires literature and literature inspires music.

Essential Questions:

- How does music inspire literature? (Addresses goals 1.02 and 5.01)
- How does literature inspire music? (Addresses goals 1.02 and 5.01)
- How do music and words create tone and mood? (Addresses goals 1.02 and 5.01)
- What are the various kinds of music? (Addresses goal 1.02)
- How has music changed over time? (Addresses goal 1.02)
- What kinds of music do kids like best? (Addresses goals 1.02 and 5.01)

Skills and Knowledge:

- Writing a problem-solution essay (Addresses goals 6.01, 6.02, and 3.02)
- Decision making and how to reach a consensus (Addresses goal 1.03)
- Brainstorming KWL (Addresses goal 1.03)
- Research skills (Addresses goal 2.02)
- Critical reading skills (especially plot and theme analysis) (Addresses goals 1.02 and 5.01)
- Creating a script (Addresses goals 1.02, 6.01, and 6.02)
- Listening and speaking skills (Addresses goals 1.03, 6.01, and 6.02)
- Interpretation skills (Addresses goals 1.02 and 5.01)
- Knowledge of tone and mood (Addresses goals 1.02 and 5.01)
- Ability to think metaphorically (Addresses goals 1.02 and 5.01)
- Connecting concrete ideas (melody and instrument choice) with abstract concepts (characterization, theme, mood, and tone) (Addresses goals 1.02 and 5.01)
- How analogy works (Addresses goals 1.02 and 5.01)

Assessment by Teacher:

- Problem-solution essay (evaluated by state rubric)
- Learning Styles Survey "What Kind of Music Instrument Are You?" (evaluated by teacher and used to group students)
- Group work on adaptation of "Synectics" (evaluated by teacher)
- Assignment sheet on how animals and tone and mood are reflected through musical instruments and melody (evaluated by teacher)
- Radio play performance (evaluated by teacher check list)
- Open-ended projects (evaluated by consensus rubric)
- Short answer test on excerpts from *The Jungle Book* (evaluated by teacher)

Assessment by Students:

♦ Each student determines his/her own assessment method.

Examples include: a brochure explaining the history of music, a rock and roll band that showed how an original poem can be set to music (literature inspires music), a musical presentation of the various kinds of music with an accompanying survey to determine kids' favorite type of music, and others.

Activities:

Day 1:

I convened a meeting of my sixth grade Language Arts students to determine our next unit of study. They became embattled in a choice between "Music" and "Heritage." Because of this battle, I had to assign a writing assignment to determine which theme would prevail. This writing assignment, which posed the problem: "Which unit should we study, music or heritage?" fit in perfectly with my curriculum, which was that students should write problem-solution essays.

Day 2:

I did not have to beg students to write, they proudly brought in their essays for the voting process. I put them in groups and asked them to take turns reading their papers to fellow group members in order to "elect" the best paper with the best solution. I chose the groups based on a balance of writing ability. Each group elected a student's paper to come before a whole-class vote. Each elected representative came before the class and read their papers to all of us. After they read, I asked them to leave the room while we voted. The winning paper determined how we would choose the unit. "Music" won.

Day 3:

I put the word "Music" on the board and we brainstormed what students knew about music and especially how music related to Language Arts. Later that day, I also got a list of what instruments students played by asking them to come to the board and write their instrument list beside their name. Next we determined the big idea: "Music inspires literature and literature inspires music." We made a list of several essential questions such as: What are the many kinds of music? How has music changed throughout time? As usual, I used two grouping strategies: one self-selected and the other selected through the use of a learning styles survey. I told students they could form their own groups based on their interests in the essential questions. I gave them time in class to discuss a project idea with their group. I asked them to fill out a Project Proposal form (see p. 43) that explained their project. In addition to allowing students to complete an open-ended project related to the music theme, I began to determine what kinds of assessments and learning activities *I* would use to teach this unit. I decided to use an excerpt from *The Jungle Book* by Rudyard Kipling because I knew the classical diction and syntax would stretch my students intellectually; I also had enough copies for the whole class to use and a CD with a classical music version of it. I also decided to use this unit to prompt my students to think more metaphorically and creatively.

Day 4:

At the beginning of this class, I gave students a survey I adapted from Katherine Butler (see Chapter 4 on grouping students by four, p. 82) called "What Kind of Instrument Are You?' in order to group them for a creative activity. On this survey students found out if they were strings (imaginative), percussion (investigative), keyboard (realistic), or brass (analytical). Most students were either imaginative or investigative. After I grouped students, we talked about the results of the survey and began to connect the concrete idea of music with the abstract idea of characterization and tone. This activity was the beginning of an adaptation of an activity called "Synectics." Go to http://edweb.sdsu.edu/Courses/ET650_OnLine/MAPPS/Synectics.html for further instruction on this highly creative activity that promotes the use of analogy and metaphorical and creative thinking. In their groups, students began the first step, "describe your topic." I asked them to choose a recorder to record their answer to this assignment: describe music. As groups finished, they turned in their recorded answers and began meeting with their "interest groups." I met with each self-selected interest group to go over their "Project Proposals." Everyone picked an excellent method of addressing a variety of the essential questions. Many of them addressed the most concrete question: What are the various types of music?

Day 5:

At the beginning of this class we did the next step in the Synectics activity, "create direct analogies." I asked students to connect music with animals to determine how animals and music are alike. Students brainstormed in groups with one of them recording the groups' answers. They turned the work in for teacher evaluation. This activity got them ready to do the next activity. For the whole class, I played an excerpt from classical music versions of Rudyard Kipling's *The Jungle Book* to show students how music was inspired by literature (Rozsa, 1996). Most students were familiar with the story because of the Disney movie, so that they were able to understand the basic story that preceded the excerpts that I was going to ask them to read. I developed a study guide that asked students to record their ideas about how the composer described the animals in the story using musical instruments and melody. I also asked them to determine the tone and mood created by the music.

We discussed their findings, and students turned in this work for evaluation.

Day 6:

In groups, I asked students to take step 3, "describe personal analogies." In this activity, students *became* an animal that was a musical instrument. They described themselves and some drew pictures. For instance, we had a violin crane, a trumpet rhinoceros, and many more. This brought lots of giggling. Next we met as a whole class to develop a consensus rubric for the open-ended projects. After we finished this whole class activity, I divided students into two teams and asked them to get with a partner or in a small group to read their assigned excerpt from *The Jungle Book*. I also demonstrated for students how to make a "flow chart" (boxes with arrows showing a progression in the story) of the story and a chart for the main characters that included what musical instrument might best represent that character. I also asked students to identify scenes in which characters showed anger, fear, or love.

Here is the character chart:

Character	Description	Musical instrument that would best represent the character	Melody type that would best represent the character
Baloo	A big friendly bear, Mowgli's advisor	A horn	A slow and lumbering happy melody

Day 7:

I did not complete the Synectics work by asking students to identify "compressed conflicts," "create a new direct analogy," and finally "reexamine the new topic." I felt these steps were beyond the scope of our needs for this unit. Also, students needed time to read with their partners and complete the "flow map" and character charts for their reading of the excerpts from *The Jungle Book*.

Day 8:

Students continued to read and outline the story in a workshop fashion.

Day 9:

Students continued to read and outline the story.

Day 10:

Final day for group work and reading and outlining the story.

Days 11 to 15:

I asked students to vote on whether they wanted to make the excerpts from *The Jungle Book* into a radio play or a stage play. They voted to make it a radio play. On each team, we had script-writers, musicians, and actors. Students worked for one week to plan and implement this radio show. The scripts were excellent, student actors practiced, and then read their parts for the performance, and student musicians practiced and then played original melodies that represented the main characters in the story on instruments such as the violin, keyboard, cello, dulcimer, trumpet, drum, and guitar. Each team performed a show for the other team, and we recorded the results, which we also listened to as a whole class. Everyone had a part and both shows were exceptional.

Day 16:

Students presented their open-ended projects. One group of boys developed a rock and roll band, wrote a song, and performed it for the class. Two students made brochures explaining the history of music, other students made posters and presentations that included results of student surveys and the playing of excerpts from various styles of music.

Day 17:

Students finished presenting projects and took a short answer test on the excerpts from *The Jungle Book.* We then addressed the other part of the "big idea," "Music inspires Literature." I played an excerpt from a classical piece by Gabriel Fauré, called "Pavone," (from *The Most Relaxing Classical Music Album in the World…Ever!* Virgin Records [March 30, 1999]). Then I played a song called "Angels Cry" by The Kennedys (*Angel Fire* Philo/Pgd. [Sept. 15, 1998]) to show how a person can take a melody and write words for it. I assigned students to think of a melody and write a poem to that melody. They loved sharing these in class on Day 18.

Consensus Rubric for Open-Ended Project on Music Unit

Category	Level 1	Level 2	Level 3	Level 4
Organization	Project lacks clear and thoughtful organization so that the audience is confused or cannot understand the answer or answers to the essential question or questions.	Project has flaws in organization so that the answers to the essential question or questions are not clear and thorough. There are some parts of the project that show a lack of organization.	Project is organized to answer one or more essential questions. Organization is mostly logical and shows evidence of thoughtful planning.	Project is organized to clearly and thoroughly answer one or more essential questions from the unit. Organization is logical and shows clear evidence of high-level thinking processes.
Originality	Project shows evidence of plagiarism or other copying. It has very little if any evidence of created information or ideas.	Project is mostly a restatement of someone or some other group's ideas and information. Very few elements of the project are created by the student or students.	Project is mostly creative expression by the student or students. Student or students may include some paraphrasing or use of clip art or art constructed by others as part of their project.	Project is constructed and created by the student or students or is a creative arrangement or synthesis of research data. Art (visual or performance) is either created by student or creatively arranged by the student.

Content	Project's content is minimal and does not sufficiently answer the essential question. It may include several inaccuracies.	Project's content leaves some important ideas out and does not sufficiently answer the essential question. It skims the surface of the topic. It may include some inaccurate information.	Project's content covers the essential question sufficiently. It includes adequate depth to cover the question. All information and ideas are accurate.	Project's content accurately and thoroughly covers the essential question beyond the expected. It includes depth and complexity of information and ideas.
Presentation	Presentation is significantly too long or too short. Presenting flaws prevent the audience from understanding the project's content.	Presentation is either too long or too short. Presenters fidget or have other verbal flaws that distract from the overall effect of the presentation.	Presentation timing may be somewhat too long or somewhat too short. Presenters maintain appropriate eye contact, but fail to develop a charismatic relationship with the audience. Presenters may fidget slightly or use one too many "ums" or other verbal flaw like talking too fast.	Presentation timing is perfect for the amount of information. Presenters develop a charismatic relationship with the audience. Presenter(s) speak clearly and do not fidget or say "um" too much.

Some analysis of this unit: I allowed some "what" or fact-based questions for this unit to allow my students to get *their* questions answered. I determined that they actually wanted to learn some facts about music; however, most of the questions were concept based. The unit I planned, although heavily process-based in terms of creating and performing, assured that through analysis of the story, students could also explore the concepts of fear, love, and anger expressed as written *or* as musical tone. Thus, students *experienced* the connection between written (literature) and musical expression providing students the potential to inspire the creative process in both directions. Through their projects and other activities, they looked at how music inspires literature and literature inspires music. For example, they saw how music or melody can become a creative song and how music inspires writers to discuss it in nonfiction forms of literary expression.

In general, this unit was highly successful. They also experienced how literature can become music and how music and language have similarities. Through the process we built our community of learners, students read a challenging work of literature, and they demonstrated excellent reading, writing, research, and presentation skills. This unit took less than one month.

Student-Led Conferences

Another way for students to be involved in their learning is through the student-led conference process. This process has become a popular method for getting students metacognitively involved in the process of learning. It encourages students to take responsibility for their own learning because it requires students to lead conferences about their work with their parents and, in some cases, with their teachers. There are various methods for implementing student-led conferences. You can find a wealth of resources by searching this topic through Google or other web directories.

I have used student-led conferences with great success. Here is a step-by-step guide explaining how to design and implement student-led conferences at school.

Step 1: Decide how you will give credit to students for completing the student-led conference process. It takes some time for students to set goals, gather materials, and meet with their parents; therefore, at least one teacher should give students a grade or points for successfully completing the process.

Step 2: Provide some kind of orientation or training to help students learn the importance of student-led conferences and to teach them the skills they will need to implement the conference. You may provide a printed script for students as the one provided here, or you may let students decide how they will present their information to their parents. Some schools videotape appropriate student-led conferences as models for students and some have a teacher or counselor designated to allow students time to role-play the process. It is important to make sure students have access to any important test scores and that they are encouraged to develop a portfolio of their work during the school year.

Student-Led Conference Script

Say to parents:

Thank you for coming to my conference. I will be leading this conference in which I will show you a selection of my work for each of my core academic classes and elective classes. I will also tell you how I believe I have performed in these classes. Finally, I will review my standardized test scores and talk to you about how I plan to improve my achievement level.

You can expect me to give an honest assessment of my progress, and what I will do to be successful the rest of the school year. We can discuss my strengths and weaknesses and discuss my goals for the rest of the year.

At the end of the conference if you feel you still have questions you would like to address to a specific teacher, please fill out the index card on the table and give it to… (counselor or facilitator). The card should have my name, your name, a phone number, and a brief explanation of what you need to discuss.

Do you have any questions so far?

First, I will show you the Reading/English/Language Arts work that I brought. (Show your parents the pieces of work you brought. Suggestions: writing samples, quizzes, tests, a project. Make a list here of what you have placed in your portfolio.)

Now I will tell you how I feel I am doing in Reading/English/Language Arts and my goals. (Write a brief reflection and at least three goals for Reading/English/Language Arts.)

My grade for Reading/English/Language Arts is _____.

Do you have any questions or comments about this work? (Record parents answers here.)

Next I will show you my Math work. (Suggestions: major tests, quizzes, homework sample. Make a list of what you have included in your portfolio.)

Now I will tell you how I feel I am doing in Math and what my goals are.

My math grade is _____.

Do you have any questions or comments about math? (Record parent's answers.)

Next I will show you my Science work. (Suggestions: notebook, quizzes, major tests, projects, labs. Make a list of what you have included in your portfolio.)

Now I will tell you how I feel I am doing in Science and what my goals are:

My grade in Science is _____.

Do you have any questions or comments about Science? (Record their responses.)

Next I will show you my Social Studies/History work. (Suggestions: notebook, major project, quizzes, major tests. List what you have included.)

Now I will tell you how I feel I am doing in Social Studies/History and what my goals are.

My grade in Social Studies/History is _____.

Do you have any questions or comments about Social Studies/History? (Record their responses.)

Now I will tell you how I feel I am doing in my electives and what my goals are.

My grades in my electives are as follows:

_____ _____
_____ _____
_____ _____
_____ _____

Do you have any questions or comments about electives? (Record their responses.)

Last, I will show you my standardized test scores from last year. [See standardized test report(s).]

These are my plans and goals for improving my scores:

Do you have any questions or comments about my goals and plans? (Record parent's questions and comments.)

Thank you for participating in my conference. Please complete the "Parent Comments" form with me now.

Parent Comments

Dear Parent,

Thank you for participating in your child's conference. We hope this experience was as rewarding for you and your child as the process was for our teachers. Please take a few moments to complete the following statements with your child. Thanks again for helping.

I was proud of you for

Keep up the good work on

I will help you with

Additional comments

Parent(s) Signature(s): _____

_____

Student Signature: _____

Date: _____

Student-Led Parent Letter

Step 3: Send letter home to parents explaining the student-led process to them.

Here is an example of a letter:

Date: _____

Dear Parents:

Please sign up to attend a student-led conference for the purpose of setting goals and making plans with your child as we begin the year. Students will lead conferences by sharing products and test scores from English/Language Arts, Social Studies/History, Science, and Math. They will also share their work from their electives. Parents and students will also look at last year's standardized test scores in order to set goals for this year. These conferences will help students take responsibility for their own learning and they will also help parents understand their child's perception of his or her strengths and weakness in academic and elective classes.

Because these conferences focus strongly on students' taking responsibility for their achievement, teachers will not be involved in them; however, you will have a chance to sign up for a parent-teacher conference if you would like. I will be available to answer questions and to facilitate these student-led conferences.

Please see the enclosed schedule to sign up for a conference. If you cannot come to the school during the allotted times, we are going to allow students to conduct conferences at home. They will get credit for conducting the conference at home if they get your written feedback and signature. We hope we will have 100% participation in this rewarding activity.

Conferences will be held during the school day from 7:40 to 2:00. See the specific dates for your child's grade level. Contact (insert Counselor or Facilitator's Name): _____ at _____.

Contact me if you have any questions or concerns. I will send a note by your child verifying your meeting time and place.

Sincerely,

(Counselor or Facilitator's Name)
Cc: Principals and Teachers

Step 4: Determine how you will conduct the conferences at school. (Note: I also allowed students to do conferences at home as long as their parents filled in the blanks and signed off that their child had conducted the conference.) In some cases grade-level teams may want to have an evening during which students lead their conferences, or someone else, such as a counselor, could coordinate the conferences by finding space and scheduling parents to come in for them.

I coordinated student-led conferences by having parents sign up to come in at certain times. I found space in the media center and developed a pass for the student to be released from class to meet with their parents for their conference. I was available if parents had questions for certain teachers or wanted to schedule a parent-teacher conference based on what they heard from their child. This process was truly exciting. I watched parents and their children discussing the child's portfolio and truly seeming to enjoy this process. Occasionally parents were interested in scheduling time to talk to their child's teachers, but for the most part, they were satisfied with what their child presented.

There are some situations that are not resolved or best handled through student-led conferences. If a student is failing or is a constant behavior problem, teachers may need to conduct parent, teacher, student, administrator conferences to deal with these difficult issues. The goal of student-led conferences is not about focusing on teachers' perceptions of students' learning. It is to allow students to focus on their own learning by setting their own learning goals, interpreting their progress, and determining the direction they need to take to address those goals.

Step 5: Make sure to give students credit for conducting their conference. When I was responsible for this event at my school. I evaluated the student's portfolios and how well they and their parents completed the process. I was truly impressed with how invested students and their parents were in this process.

Student-Led Questioning:
Seminar Discussion and "Best Answer" Questioning

Another way students can be more involved in their learning is to use seminar discussion and group questioning strategies.

Seminar Discussion

Students take responsibility for their own learning when they participate in seminar discussions. Many teachers enjoy using seminar discussion groups to discuss issues presented through text or video presentation. Socratic seminar and other seminar methods require students to do the following:

- ♦ Ask and answer open-ended questions,
- ♦ Speak without being called on by the teacher,
- ♦ Respect the speaker,
- ♦ Use standard English,
- ♦ Reference the text or video to substantiate points when answering questions.

Most teachers train students to write questions for seminar discussions. For me, the most useful question-writing model is "Three Levels of Questions." I teach students that Level 1 questions are "right there" in the text. Level 2 questions require them to make inferences and draw conclusions or "read between the lines." Level 3 questions go "beyond the text," and a good beginning question stem for these questions is: "What does this…teach us about…?"

In seminar discussions, students take a great deal of responsibility for learning. Seminar discussions are wonderful venues for requiring students to answer open-ended questions that require divergent reasoning ability (thinking of many *possible* answers). But what about standardized testing that requires students to use convergent reasoning (finding *best* answers) to answer challenging questions? Divergent reasoning can work against tests that require convergent reasoning, and these kinds of *best* answer tests comprise most of the "tests that count" in our current education systems. Even if students' answers to open-ended questions are "tied to a text," students still need a great deal of practice using their convergent reasoning skills if they want to achieve on standardized tests. Often teachers do not align their own questioning with how students are tested. What follows is a method for using the jigsaw group method to train students to take responsibility for writing "best answer" questions that require convergent reasoning.

Teaching Students to Write Best Answer Questions

Big Idea: Learning how to write questions that require determining *best* answers and possible answers that are *not best* will address metacognition and improve students' higher-order thinking skills.

Essential Question: How does a person write *best answer* questions that are based on four higher-level thinking categories: cognition, interpretation, critical stance, and connections?

Skills:

Critical reading skills

Collaborative group skills

Writing questions for four categories: cognition, interpretation, critical stance, and connections.

Knowledge: The four categories of questions

End-of-Grade (EOG) Standardized test format

EOG: style of answers (i.e., no "all of the above" and no negative answers)

Acceptable evidence of learning: Each student will demonstrate the ability to accurately write questions with accompanying answers for each of the four categories and on a variety of literary genre. The teacher will give feedback and opportunities for more practice based on level of achievement.

Activities: (This lesson follows an analysis of benchmark test results)

Lesson 1

Materials needed: "Question Stems" handout and a short literary selection (poem, short story, or other)

Room: Arranged for whole class instruction.

Objective: Read a selection and write one question per Category: Cognition, Interpretation, Critical Stance, and Connections.

Step 1: Students take a copy of the "Question Stems" handout as they enter the room. Instruct them to read it on their own.

Step 2: Go over the "Question Stems" handout as a whole class. Review the handout to make sure students understand all concepts addressed on that handout.

Step 3: Ask students to find the selection in their textbook or hand out the selection. Tell students that they will be practicing writing EOG-style questions based on this selection.

Step 4: Either read the selection aloud or have students read it silently.

Step 5: Ask students to write one cognition question based on the selection.

Step 6: Ask student volunteers to share their question and answers to check for understanding.

Step 7: Continue this process for all four categories.

Step 8: Collect the students' work and evaluate it to determine if they are on the right track. Give students feedback about their work, so that they might improve it if necessary. Writing these questions is not easy; therefore, once students have the basic idea, the next step is to practice more but in collaboration with others.

Lessons 2 to 5 (Jigsaw)

Materials needed: A selection for each student to read.

Room: Arranged for cooperative learning. Students are divided into "home groups" of four (if you cannot do that, go with some fives, not threes, fives can double up, i.e., the four and five both go to the "question-writing group"). If a student is absent, the "home group" indicates no questions from that student on the quiz.

Objectives: Students will work collaboratively to write EOG-style questions. Students will take a student-made EOG-style quiz.

Step 1:   Have group assignments listed on the board. Ask students to sit with their assigned "home group." Ask each home group to number off one to four (if five, double up).

Step 2:   Ask each home group to read a selection and talk about it. All groups will not finish at the same time; therefore, you need to prepare students to talk about the selection rather than taking the time to socialize.

Step 3:   After all groups have finished reading the selection, show students how they will move into four corners of the room. Ones go in one corner, twos in another, and so forth. (You may need to practice this movement if your students are not good at getting into groups.)

Step 4:   After students have formed their "question writing group," write on the board which category each group should be responsible for writing questions and answers about. For example: Ones write cognition questions, twos write interpretation questions, threes write critical stance questions, and fours write connections questions. Ask students to write two EOG-style questions for their assigned category. Review, if necessary, what that means based on the previous lesson. Make sure to remind students to carefully disguise "right" answers so that "home group" members cannot see them.

Step 5:   After all students have finished writing questions and answers, ask them to go back to their "home groups."

Step 6:   When students are in "home groups," ask them to number their papers one to six on the back of the paper on which they have written their questions.

Step 7:   Students take turns asking their questions and having their home group members write the answers.

Step 8:   Students go over right answers. (Note: Allow students to challenge poor questions. Tell them if they make a convincing argument explaining why the question is unfair, you (the teacher) will consider not counting a wrong answer against them.)

Step 9:   Make sure all students turn in their work.

Step 10: Grade the work as follows:
All correct = A+
One wrong = A–
Two wrong = B
Three wrong = C
Four wrong = D
Five- six wrong = F
If students write poor answers, I lower the grade to a minus, for example, a B becomes a B–. If they make an A–, that grade becomes a B.

Step 11:   Give students their papers back in a timely manner. (Next class is best.) Repeat steps 2 to 11, 3 more times so that all students will have a chance to practice each question category. Use a different genre for each session.

The following information addresses aspects of "Student-Led Unit Planning:"

Robin Fogarty's THEMES

Robin Fogarty (1995) has a long list of themes in her book *Best Practices for the Learner Centered Classroom* (p. 19). She also uses a curriculum-designing framework called THEMES (p. 20) in which she suggests the following:

Think of Themes: There are hundreds.

Hone the list: Make the list fit your content or grade-level concepts.

Extrapolate the criteria: Criteria: a useful theme is one that it is relevant to students, the resources to teach it are available, it is broad enough to integrate with all content areas, it is engaging to both students and teachers.

Manipulate the theme: Use the theme to generate important essential questions.

Expand into activities: Think of activities that are within your content or across your content that would be useful to address the theme.

Select goals and assessments: Determine learning goals and how to assess them.

Fogarty's method is excellent and adaptable to allow students' choices.

H. Lynn Erickson's Concept-Based Curriculum Ideas

H. Lynn Erickson (2002) also has some excellent ideas about developing theme-based/concept-based curriculum and instruction. Although her model is similar to the Wiggins-McTighe (1998) model, she includes some interesting differences. One of the differences is in her explanation of themes and concepts. She provides an excellent process for planning concept-based instruction that helps students and teachers move beyond the facts. Some of her ideas that I find extremely helpful are:

♦ Start with a theme that is discipline-based. For example: The formation of government in third world countries.

♦ After you have your theme, determine the major concept that will provide the *lens* through which you examine that theme. She defines a *concept* as an organizing term that is abstract, universal, timeless, and expressed in one or two words. Some concepts are "macro concepts" that apply to all disciplines. Other concepts apply to only certain disciplines and should not be "forced" to apply if they do not. Example of a macro concept is *change*.

◆ Next, write generalizations that are sentences following the statement "students will learn that...," for example, the *change* in *medical issues* affects the *formation* of *governments* in third world countries. The concepts are italicized. Avoid generalization statements that use the verbs *is, are,* and *have.*

◆ After writing generalizations, determine essential questions that become deeper and more meaningful for learning as you ask the question "so what?" Use "how" and "why" questions rather than "what" questions if you want to move beyond fact learning. Example: How are medical issues related to the formation of a government?

◆ After essential questions, teachers examine what students must know and do and will learn to know and do as they answer their essential questions and examine their theme.

◆ Next teachers plan engaging activities that will address these questions and concepts.

◆ Finally, the teacher will determine a "performance task" that answers these questions: *What* concept will the performance address, or what question will the student answer? *Why* will they address this area or answer this question?

◆ How will students demonstrate that they have addressed the concept or answered the question(s)? Example: *What:* Explain how medical issues affect the formation of governments in third world counties. *Why:* To understand how changing medical conditions (i.e., HIV, sleeping sickness) can affect political power. *How:* Demonstrate understanding by writing an essay that compares two third world countries in terms of how their governments have or have not been affected by changing medical issues.

I also found these statements interesting:

◆ English/Language Arts is not concept based; it is based on students' learning skills and processes. Literature is the content and concept-based area of the language arts (p. 8). Erickson says that students' ability to use the language arts (reading, writing, speaking, listening) forms the basis for all disciplines and should be a consideration for them all.

◆ Math is often decontextualized and therefore, loses its sense of real world application. Concept-based instruction can help math teachers show the power of math in the real world.

I highly recommend her book, *Concept-Based Curriculum and Instruction: Teaching Beyond the Facts.*

Summary

Getting students involved in their own learning is a must in the democratic differentiated classroom model. This chapter has explained how you can increase student's metacognitive processing by implementing three major strategies:

- Student-Led Unit Planning,
- Student-Led Conferences, and
- Student-Led Questioning.

4

How to Group Students for Differentiated Instruction

One of the most important aspects of the democratic differentiated classroom is the ability of the teacher to effectively group students or help students group themselves for learning. How do you assess students' learning and thinking styles in order to flexibly group them? This chapter provides examples and explains methods for flexibly grouping students in order to differentiate, and thus, maximize students' learning potential. The groupings are based on:

- ♦ Learning styles (in groups of threes, fours, and fives)
- ♦ Interests
- ♦ Ability or readiness
- ♦ Student-selected groups
- ♦ Personality based groups

This chapter also explains how I use Gardner's Multiple Intelligences (MI) to help students make project choices.

Learning Styles

Teachers who have experimented with differentiating instruction know that there are many ways to group students. Several theorists offer valuable information that can be implemented in the classroom. There are many useful surveys and inventories that can help students and teachers determine learning style preferences. Some of these learning styles inventories divide learning preferences by groups of three, four, or five. I will explain and give examples of the grouping by learning style strategies I find most useful.

Number Grouped by:	Type
Three	Auditory, Visual, Kinesthetic
	Sternberg's Triarchic Theory
Four	Anthony Gregorc
	Katherine Butler
	David Kolb
	Bernice McCarthy
	Carl Jung
Five	Gardner's Entry Points

Grouping by Three

1. **Auditory, Visual, and Kinesthetic**

   Many teachers find it easiest to group into three categories: auditory, visual, and kinesthetic learners; however, your class may not have equal numbers of students in each of these categories. Therefore, you need to be careful not to make lessons that assume equal distribution. Learning Channel Preferences is an excellent assessment tool for determining students' learning style.

Learning Channel Preference

The "Learning Channel Preference" is a helpful checklist adapted from Dr. Lynn O'Brien (1990).

Learning Channel Preference

Read each sentence carefully and consider whether or not it applies to you.

3 = often applies, 2 = sometimes applies, 1 = almost never applies, 0 = never applies

Add up the numbers. The channel with the highest score is your learning channel preference.

A	Channel _____
_____	1. When I read, I listen to the word in my head or read aloud.
_____	2. To memorize something, it helps me to say what I am trying to learn over and over to myself.
_____	3. I need to talk about things to understand them.
_____	4. I don't need to take notes in class.
_____	5. I remember what people have said, better than what they were wearing.
_____	6. I like to record things to listen to on tape.
_____	7. I'd rather hear a lecture on something rather than have to read about it.
_____	8. I can easily follow a speaker even when I am not watching that person talk.
_____	9. I talk to myself when I'm solving a problem or writing.
_____	10. I prefer to have someone tell me how to do something rather than to read the directions myself.
_____	A Total

B   **Channel** _____

_____ 1. I don't like to read or listen to directions; I'd rather just start doing.

_____ 2. I learn best when I am shown how to do something and then have the opportunity to do it.

_____ 3. I can study better when music is playing.

_____ 4. I solve problems more often by trial-and-error, than when using a step-by-step approach.

_____ 5. My desk and/or locker look disorganized.

_____ 6. I need frequent breaks while studying.

_____ 7. I take notes but never go back to read them.

_____ 8. I do not become easily lost, even in strange surroundings.

_____ 9. I think better when I have the freedom to move around; I have a hard time studying at a desk.

_____ 10. When I can't think of a specific word, I'll use my hands a lot and call something a "thing-a-ma-jig."

_____ B   Total

C   **Channel** _____

_____ 1. I enjoy doodling and even my notes have lots of pictures, arrows, and other marks on them.

_____ 2. I remember something better if I write it down.

_____ 3. When I am trying to remember a telephone number or something new, it helps me to picture it in my head.

_____ 4. When I am taking a test, I can "see" the textbook page and the correct answer on it.

_____ 5. Unless I write down directions, I am likely to get lost or arrive late.

_____ 6. It helps me to look at the person speaking. It keeps me focused.

_____ 7. I can clearly picture things in my head.

_____ 8. It's hard for me to understand what a person is saying when there is background noise.

_____ 9. It's difficult for me to understand a joke when I hear it.

_____ 10. It's easier for me to get work done in a quiet place.

_____ C   Total

Key: Channel A = Auditory Learner, Channel B = Kinesthetic Learner, Channel C = Visual Learner

How to Use This Survey as a Lesson to Group Students

Materials (Prepared in Advance): Have pieces of poster paper labeled and ready to go. Because you do not know how many of each learner you will have, you should have several posters already labeled as illustrated below.

♦ Have markers available at each poster.

♦ Have your "Learning Channel Preference" handout ready to go.

♦ Set up the room to accommodate movement and flexible grouping.

Auditory Learners

What does it mean to be an auditory learner?

Visual Learners

What does it mean to be a visual learner?

Kinesthetic Learners

What does it mean to be a kinesthetic learner?

Note: You may have only one of a category, a couple, or most of the class in one category. Be prepared to adjust where you ask groups to go. You can place posters in various corners of the room, at various tables, on the floor, out in the hall.

Step 1: Tell students that you are giving them a survey to determine how they like to learn. Make sure you share with them that this survey only shows tendencies, that it is not a matter of labeling them or categorizing them for life. Tell them that some people change their styles as they get older. And that everyone needs to be able to learn in all of the channels if they want to be successful in school.

Step 2: Hand out the "Learning Channel Survey" and ask students to complete it. Tell them that as soon as they complete the survey, they should go to the poster that reflects the result of their survey. In case a student has no clear preference, ask them to choose the one that seems strongest of the three.

Step 3: Tell students that when they get to the appropriate poster, they should use the graffiti method to answer the question on the chart. The graffiti method means they might write words, phrases, sentences, draw pictures and other graphics in any organized or random manner they may choose.

Step 4: After students complete their group posters, ask them to choose a presenter to explain the poster to the whole class.

Grouping Ideas

Once you know each student's preferred learning channel, you may use that data to group students and to plan lessons. Grouping ideas include the following:

♦ Make groups of three that include one of each learning style. (This is idealistic because your class will most likely not have a balance.) When groups receive assignments, the auditory person can be in charge of listening, the visual person can read and interpret text, and the kinesthetic person can take the notes.

♦ Make groups of students of like style and ask them to respond to questions from their strength. For example: Auditory groups can use an oral presentation of their solution. Visual groups can draw pictures and graphs to present their solution. Kinesthetic groups can use role play, games, and other active methods of presenting their solution.

General Ideas

Now that you know the makeup of your class, you know how many students represent each of the three learning styles. You can depend on the fact that you will have a number of kinesthetic learners in the earlier grades, but that as students mature there may be more of a mix. You will most likely have students who represent each learning style. You must be committed to presenting information in all three styles and to letting students show you what they know in these styles. In terms of presenting information, you and your students need to speak, show, and act out almost all information. This sounds difficult, but it is not. Most teachers know that as they give information, they need to use their voices and a visual representation, and most teachers have learned to "model" what they do. Modeling can include "practicing."

Practicing is Kinesthetic

All teachers can address the needs of kinesthetic learners if they use the idea of practicing. For instance, if you want students to follow a specific procedure, you need to take time to have them go through the motions involved in that process. This practice idea applies to elementary through high school students. In many cases, even adults need "to experience" a process before they understand how to follow it. The more complex the process, the younger the students, the more practice they need. You may practice by having everyone go through the steps or you may have a representative group model the steps for the class. Practicing all kinds of student processes can make learning much easier for those who learn through the work their bodies do.

The Kinesthetic Lecture

Another way to address the needs of kinesthetic learners is to use "the kinesthetic lecture." This just means that any new information or skill you want to introduce to your students can be acted out, not necessarily by you, but by your kinesthetic learners. You can take any concept, even the most abstract, and assign students to take the roles of those concepts. For example, when I teach the concepts of claim, data, and warrant, which are types of sentences in argumentative writing, I have one student represent "claim," three students represent "data," and one represents "warrant." As I read a short explanation of what each of these terms mean, I have the students assigned to these roles act them out for the class. When I want to remind students about the meaning of these terms, I can say, "You remember this term; the part was played by...." More examples of creating kinesthetic lessons are presented in Chapter 5.

Writing is Kinesthetic

If you want to present new information to students in a minilecture, you might remind them that listening to the teacher is auditory, writing the notes is kinesthetic, and seeing the notes is visual. Informing students about the importance of addressing all learning channels to maximize learning potential addresses the use of metacognitive skills.

2. **Sternberg's Thinking Styles Model**

Sternberg's most recent book explains his three types of thinking styles using a government metaphor. He says that thinking styles fit into the same categories that our founding fathers determined were important to democracy. In order to assure the best functioning of society, these founders divided our government into three branches: legislative, executive, and judicial. Sternberg says this division is perfectly aligned with "thinking styles." For instance, some people are most closely aligned with creating or making laws or ideas, some are more aligned with executing those laws or ideas, and some are more aligned with judging how those laws or ideas are implemented. Sternberg says that no one thinking style is superior to another and that people might draw upon various styles depending on their situation; however, he says that knowing your dominant thinking style can help you find the "best fit" in learning and in making decisions in your life. Here is my interpretation of how Sternberg's ideas might mesh with Gardner's Multiple Intelligences.

Triarchic Thinking Styles/MI	Creative Legislative	Realistic Executive	Critical Judicial
Verbal/Linguistic	Writes novels, plays, nonfiction, poems, teaches English	Writes for a newspaper, writes reports for organizations	Literary critic
Mathematical/ Logical	Manages people in creative endeavors, entrepreneurial	CEO of a company, lawyer who implements ideas for clients	Business analyst, stock analyst
Body Kinesthetic	Director, dance choreographer, coach	Dancer, actor, player	Arts critic, sports analyst
Musical	Composer	Musician	Music Critic
Spatial	Visual artist	Commercial artist	Art critic, art history professor, museum director
Naturalist	Director of parks and recreation	Park ranger	Environmental advocate

Grouping Students Using Sternberg: A Lesson

Materials: "A Story of Three Students" and the "Your Thinking Style" handout.

Objective: Students discover their thinking style preference in order to form inquiry teams.

Instruction: Tell the students that you will be grouping them according to their thinking style preference, and that first you are going to read them a short story of three students.

A Story of Three Students

This is a story about thinking styles inspired by the work of Richard Sternberg and based on the idea that people have three different styles of thinking. As you listen to this story you need to think about the idea that no one of these styles is better than the other, and that you might actually use a certain style depending on the situation. The main point is you might want to think about your preferences and abilities because having this knowledge may help you better choose how you want to learn or work.

This story is about three students. We will call them A, B, and C so that they will have no gender bias or ethnicity. Students A, B, and C all made A's all through school. When they went to college, Student A noticed that when taking a class in which the professor carefully organized the curriculum and made the learning requirements specific, this student was successful and happy. Student A continued to make As in these kinds of classes; however, if a professor gave Student A an open-ended assignment that required the student to determine how to address it or to create solutions, Student A was not as successful and was not comfortable.

Student B felt bored and restricted when professors organized the curriculum and made the learning procedures highly specific. Student B sometimes made Cs in these kinds of classes when not inspired by the work; however, if a professor gave Student B an open-ended assignment that required the student to determine how to address it and to create solutions, Student B was successful and happy.

Student C noticed that developing criteria and judging things fit well in many classes. Most professors required students to analyze and problem solve in closed or open-ended assignments. This student made As when required to use critical thinking skills and judge criteria in order to create a product or follow a professor's closely outlined curriculum. Student C was not as successful, however, if required to create something or to follow a syllabus closely if analysis and criticism were not useful.

Student A became a successful lawyer who analyzed clients' needs and implemented their ideas. Student B became a research laboratory director who determined the direction of research and supervised many graduate assistants. Student C became a judge in the local court system. All three students were highly successful in their chosen professions.

Discussion: Ask the students if they have any questions or comments about the story. After students have discussed the issue, give them the "Thinking Styles Survey." Tell students to give their completed surveys to you. Answer any questions students have as they fill out the survey.

Thinking Styles Survey

Please circle the answer that best describes you.

1. When I am studying fiction, I prefer…
    a. to make up my own story with my own characters and plot.
    b. to evaluate the author's style, to criticize the author's ideas, and to evaluate characters' actions.
    c. to show how much I know about a work of fiction by accurately and thoroughly responding to an assignment sheet constructed by the teacher.
    d. to do something else (please describe your preference in the space below).

2. When I am studying nonfiction, I prefer…

   a. to express in writing or orally, my understanding and evaluation of the work.

   b. to imagine how I would act under the same circumstances and show in a creative way that I understand the information.

   c. to show in a way determined by the teacher that I understand a certain amount of information in that work.

   d. to do something else (please describe your preference in the space below).

3. After school I usually…

   a. participate in a number of school-related clubs, organizations, or sports teams.

   b. go my own way; I do not like organized activities.

4. When I am shopping for new clothes, I prefer to buy things that

   a. are different from anything anyone else is wearing so I can create my own style.

   b. are similar to things that my closest friends are wearing.

Comments:

Adapted by S. Waterman from Sternberg, R. J. (1997). *Thinking styles.* New York: Cambridge University Press (pp. 42, 43).

Grouping Students: After you have determined the preferred thinking style of all of your students, you may group them by like-minded or various-minded criteria. As with other style preferences, you will most likely not get an equal number of each style; therefore, you need to be prepared to adjust your groups to best accommodate students' needs.

Grouping by Four

This chart is an overview of theories that group students by 4.

Theories	Theorists	Description	
Mind Styles	Anthony Gregorc	Abstract	Concrete
		Random	Sequential
		A person can be "abstract random," "concrete sequential," abstract sequential," or "concrete random."	
Learning Dimensions	Katherine Butler	Divides learners into the following categories:	
		Imaginative	Investigative
		Realistic	Analytical
Learning Styles Inventory	David Kolb	Kolb says we learn in the following four stages:	
		1. Concrete Experience: feeling (CE)	2. Reflective Observation: watching (RO)
		3. Abstract Conceptualization: thinking (AC)	4. Active Experimentation: doing (AE)
		From these stages comes Kolb's definition of four learning styles as follows:	
		Diverging (CE/RO)	Assimilating (AC/RO)
		Converging (AC/AE)	Accommodating (CE/AE)
		http://www.businessballs.com/kolblearningstyles.htm	
4 Mat	Bernice McCarthy (based on Gregorc, Butler, Kolb)	Abstract	
		Active Side	Reflective Side
		Quadrant 1: Dynamic Learner	Quadrant 2: Imaginative Learner
		Quadrant 3: Common Sense Learner	Quadrant 4: Analytic Learner
		Concrete	
		Teachers plan lessons that address each quadrant.	
Personality Styles	Carl Jung	Introvert	
		Sensing	Thinking
		Extrovert	
		Intuiting	Feeling

Myers (1985)-Briggs Type Indicator	Katharine Briggs and Isabel Briggs Myers (based on Carl Jung)	4 Scales Sensing:	
		Extroversion/Introversion (E-I)	Sensing/Intuiting (S-N)
		Thinking/Feeling (T-F)	Judging/Perceiving (J-P)
		Ex: An ENTJ is a person who is Extroverted, Intuitive, Thinking, and Judgmental.	
Four Learning Styles	Silver, Strong, Perini (2000)	Sensing (S)	Thinking (T)
		Feeling (F)	Intuition (N)
		(ST) Mastery Style	(SF) Interpersonal Style
		(NT) Understanding Style	(NF) Self-expressive Style

All of the above theorists have inventories or surveys that help people know their personality or learning style. The inventory I like to use is based on the work of Katherine Butler. Unlike most of the other inventories, it seems to be normed for students. It's called "What Kind of Fruit Are Your?"

A Lesson Idea Using Katherine Butler's Learning Styles

Katherine Butler (1987) has developed an engaging activity called "What Kind of Fruit Are You?" I found this activity in Stephen Covey, Jr.'s *Seven Habits of Effective Teens* (1998).

Materials: Adapt the survey to match your unit. For example, when I did a unit on "music" I called it "What Kind of Instrument Are You?" When I used a topic that had animals involved, I used "What Kind of Animal Are You?"

Make a station for each learning style. For example: Dogs, Cats, Horses, Birds.

Instruction: Tell students that you will be grouping them according to their learning style. Ask them to take the following survey and to report to the appropriate station when they know which fruit they are:

What Kind of Fruit Are You?

Directions: Read across each row and place a *4* in the blank for the word that best describes you. Now place a *3* in the blank for the second word that describes you best. Do the same for the final words using a *2* and a *1*. Do this for each row.

The first row is an example:

Imaginative	2	Investigative	4	Realistic	1	Analytical	3
Column One		Column Two		Column Three		Column Four	
Imaginative		Investigative		Realistic		Analytical	
Adaptable		Inquisitive		Organized		Critical	
Relating		Creating		Getting to the point		Debating	
Personal		Adventurous		Practical		Academic	
Flexible		Inventive		Precise		Systematic	
Sharing		Independent		Orderly		Sensible	
Cooperative		Competitive		Perfectionist		Logical	
Sensitive		Risk-taking		Hardworking		Intellectual	
People-person		Problem-solver		Planner		Reader	
Associate		Originate		Memorize		Think through	
Spontaneous		Charger		Wants direction		Judger	
Communicating		Discovering		Cautious		Reasoning	
Caring		Challenging		Practicing		Examining	
Feeling		Experimenting		Doing		Thinking	

Now add up your totals (don't include the example) for each column and place the totals in the blanks below

Column One		Column Two		Column Three		Column Four	
Grape		*Orange*		*Banana*		*Melon*	

Find your fruit and go to the appropriate station. Look on the back of the survey to see what it means to be this fruit. Discuss your learning style with those who join you in the station. Talk about whether this survey accurately describes you or not.

Activity: When students have completed their surveys you may have only one or two students in one or more of the categories; be prepared to adjust. If this happens let the students who are by themselves choose the next closest group. When students are in their groups, get them to discuss what having this learning style means in terms of the following chart (you might have the chart on the back of the survey).

What does Your Fruit Mean to You?

	Grapes	Oranges	Bananas	Melons
Natural abilities include:	• being reflective • being sensitive • being creative • preference for working in groups	• experimenting • being independent • being curious • creating different approaches • creating change	• planning • organizing • fact finding • following directions	• debating points of view • analyzing ideas • finding solutions • determining value or importance
Can learn best when they:	• can work and share with others • balance work with play • can communicate • are noncompetitive	• can use trial and error • can compete • produce real products • are self-directed	• have an orderly environment • have specific outcomes • can trust others to do their parts • have predictable situations	• have access to resources • can work independently • are respected for intellectual ability • follow traditional methods
May have trouble:	• giving exact answers • organizing • focusing on one thing at a time	• meeting time limits • having few options or choices • following a lecture	• understanding feelings • answering "what if" questions • dealing with opposition	• working in groups • being criticized • convincing others diplomatically
To expand their style they need to:	• pay more attention to details • be less emotional when making decisions • do not rush into things	• Delegate responsibility • be more accepting of others' ideas • learn to prioritize	• express their own feelings more • get explanations of others' views • be less rigid	• accept imperfection • consider others' feelings • consider all alternatives

Kathleen Butler has many publications and a homepage. Search on: Kathleen Butler's Homepage through Google.com.

Grouping Ideas: You may use this method to group by like-minded or un-like-minded depending on the goals for your unit. This method has been most useful in my classes after students have been grouped in other ways.

Grouping by Five

This grouping method is based on the work of Harold Gardner.

Entry Point	Description
Narrative	Learning through story: Students prefer reading, writing, discussing.
Logical/Quantitative	Learning through numbers/logic: Students prefer recording ideas graphic organizers or charts.
Foundational	Learning through theory and discovering meaning: Students prefer analyzing and determining what something means.
Aesthetic	Learning through the arts: Students prefer showing what they know through artistic talents.
Experiential	Learning through hands on: Students prefer experiencing a concept, not just hearing about it or seeing examples.

You might combine these entry points with your knowledge of students' Multiple Intelligences surveys to determine how to group students by entry points or have students choose their group based on its description. The entry points seem to be more useful as a mechanism for grouping than grouping by Multiple Intelligences (MI).

How to Group by Five

Materials: This is a cubing lesson, therefore, you must first construct the cubes. See my *Handbook on Differentiated Instruction for Middle and High School* (Northey, 2005). Use five cubes (or learning stations) with assignments differentiated by entry point emphasis. Each cube (or station) represents an entry point. Students might rotate using the cubes (or stations), you might assign students to use the cube (or station) that suits their learning style best according to an MI survey, or you might have students select a cube (or station) based on their own interest in an entry point.

The assignments you write should be based on themes or concepts you are covering.

Instruction: Ask students to get into groups and roll the cube (or read assignments listed at the station) to determine which activity they should do as a group or individually.

See the following chart for generic questions for each entry point (the blanks represent concepts you are covering in your unit):

Entry Point	Assignments for Individuals or Whole Group
Narrative	1. Tell a 2-minute story about … 2. Read a picture book (provided) about … 3. Write a paragraph that explains …. 4. Pose 3 questions for the group to discuss about … 5. Give a 1-minute speech about … 6. Write a poem about …
Logical/ Quantitative	1. Make a graph that shows … 2. Make a chart that shows … 3. Take a survey and record the results to determine … 4. Analyze this chart, graph, or map of … 5. Make a database that compares and contrasts … 6. Outline the main points of….
Foundational	1. Use induction to determine … 2. Make and test a hypothesis about … 3. Research and write a paragraph about … 4. Determine the theory behind _____ and discuss it as a group … 5. Categorize … 6. Make a timeline to show the history of …
Aesthetic	1. Draw a picture that represents … 2. Make a 3 three-dimensional representation of … 3. Write a song about … 4. Perform a skit about … 5. Choreograph a dance that shows … 6. Perform using an artistic expression as an example of …
Experiential	1. Make a game that teaches about … 2. Do an experiment that shows … 3. Play the (provided) game to learn about … 4. Make a _____ to show you understand … 5. Demonstrate how to …. 6. Find a kinesthetic method to teach …

Grouping by Interests

Grouping students by their interests is one of the best and most exciting grouping methods. It's easy to find out students' interests; you just ask them. If you are teaching thematically, it is a good idea to group students according to their interests in answering certain essential questions or according to a career interest and its relationship to the theme, or you might even allow students to work on their own theme. For instance, for the last unit of the year, I allow my students to group themselves according to the theme they have wanted to do, but that did not win in the voting process. Students choose their theme *and* how they will address it. In my *Handbook on Differentiated Instruction for Middle and High School* (Northey, 2005), I show how to use students' interests in sports, shopping, music, and visual arts to teach ratios and proportions. You might also group students based on their interest in a certain aspect or topic within your unit. Here is an example of grouping students by their interest in a science/social studies topic.

Example of Interest Groups Strategy

Unit of Study	Extreme Weather Systems (Science–Social Studies Integration)
Theme Extreme	Weather systems occur because of certain conditions, and they have an effect on people, economy, landforms, and culture.
Interest Groups	All groups will answer these questions in a presentation to the class. How does the extreme weather you are studying occur? How does it have an impact on people, economy, landforms, and culture? They will make a creative presentation to the class that will include the following: a visual and a verbal presentation, a hands-on activity, and a test on the materials that they covered. The presentation will be evaluated by check sheet.
Group #1 Hurricanes	
Materials	• Textbook articles (hard copy) or electronic found in journals, magazines, encyclopedias, or online • A hurricane film • Markers, cards, posterboard, glue
Activities	1. Discuss how to begin the inquiry process (especially how to divide the topic) 2. Inquiry: Find a variety of sources on hurricanes in the media center and computer lab. 3. Read materials and take notes. 4. Share results of inquiry and discuss how to answer the question and present information to the class.

	5. Divide tasks and create the various elements of the assignment. 6. Present to class.
Product	See syllabus with "check sheet" evaluation.

Group #2
Tornados

Materials	◆ Textbooks ◆ Articles (hard copy) or electronic found in journals, magazines, encyclopedias or online ◆ A tornado film ◆ Markers, cards, posterboard, glue
Activities	1. Discuss how to begin the inquiry process (especially how to divide the topic) 2. Inquiry: Find a variety of sources on tornados in the media center and computer lab. 3. Read materials and take notes. 4. Share results of inquiry and discuss how to answer the question and present information to the class. 5. Divide tasks and create the various elements of the assignment. 6. Present to class.
Product	See syllabus with "check sheet" evaluation.

Group #3
Extreme Rain (e.g., as in Rain Forests)

Materials	◆ Textbooks Articles (hard copy) or electronic found in journals, magazines, encyclopedias, or online ◆ A film about rain forests ◆ Markers, cards, poster board, glue
Activities	1. Discuss how to begin the inquiry process (especially how to divide the topic). 2. Inquiry: Find a variety of sources on rain forests in the media center and computer lab. 3. Read materials and take notes. 4. Share results of inquiry and discuss how to answer the question and present information to the class. 5. Divide tasks and create the various elements of the assignment. 6. Present to class.
Product	See syllabus with "check sheet" evaluation.

	Group #4 **Extreme Drought (e.g., as in desert climates)**
Materials	• Textbooks Articles (hard copy) or electronic found in journals, magazines, encyclopedias, or online • A film on deserts/drought • Markers, cards, poster board, glue
Activities	1. Discuss how to begin the inquiry process (especially how to divide the topic). 2. Inquiry: Find a variety of sources on deserts/drought in the media center and computer lab. 3. Read materials and take notes. 4. Share results of inquiry and discuss how to answer the question and present information to the class. 5. Divide tasks and create the various elements of the assignment. 6. Present to class.
Product	See syllabus with "check sheet" evaluation.
	Group #5 **Extreme cold (e.g., as in the Arctic and Antarctic)**
Materials	• Textbooks Articles (hard copy) or electronic found in journals, magazines, encyclopedias, or online • A film about the Arctic and/or Antarctic • Markers, cards, poster board, glue
Activities	1. Discuss how to begin the inquiry process (especially how to divide the topic). 2. Inquiry: Find a variety of sources on the Arctic and Antarctic in the media center and computer lab. 3. Read materials and take notes. 4. Share results of inquiry and discuss how to answer the question and present information to the class. 5. Divide tasks and create the various elements of the assignment. 6. Present to class.
Product	See syllabus with "check sheet" evaluation.

Syllabus for Extreme Weather Interest Groups

Process

1. Choose one of the following topics (write down your first choice and second choice): hurricanes, tornados, extreme rain (e.g., as in Rain Forests), extreme drought (e.g., as in desert climates), or extreme cold (e.g., as in the Arctic and Antarctic).

2. Discuss how to begin the inquiry process (especially how to divide the topic).

3. Inquiry: Find a variety of sources in the media center and computer lab.

4. Read materials and take notes.

5. Share results of inquiry and discuss how to answer the question and present information to the class.

6. Divide tasks and create the various elements of the assignment.

7. Present to class.

Products

Each group must develop the following products:

1. A visual that demonstrates the following elements:

   _____ accuracy of information
   _____ sufficiency of information
   _____ neatness
   _____ creativity
   _____ artistic design

2. An oral presentation taken from note cards. The presentation must include the following elements:

   _____ accurate information
   _____ sufficient information
   _____ audible
   _____ engaging to the audience
   _____ creative

3. A hands-on activity

   _____ engaging to the audience
   _____ helps students understand a concept of the topic
   _____ information accurate
   _____ information sufficient
   _____ creative

4. A test on the topic

   _____ accurate information

____ fair grading
____ questions related to the presentation
____ sufficient and challenging questions
____ fair questions

Grading:

Visual	=	25 points (5 points per check)
Presentation	=	40 points (8 points per check)
Hands-on activity	=	25 points (5 points per check)
Test	=	<u>10</u> points (2 points per check)
Total		100 points

Grouping by Readiness

Here is a chart of generic guidelines for determining which students may be successful in which level. You may want to collaborate with students to determine where they are most comfortable or based on your assessment of their readiness to effectively deal with certain learning challenges as follows:

Grouping Strategies by Readiness
to Effectively Deal with Various Learning Challenges

Level	Readiness Activities That Promote Failure/Frustration at This Level	Readiness Activities That Promote Achievement/ Motivation at This Level
Below Grade Level	• Too many concepts addressed by the group activity. • Too many steps needed. • Too much time spent without breaks. • Resources that require a great deal of unassisted reading and/or text with low word-to-text ratios (i.e., reading materials should have pictures to support text).	• Teacher assistance available to groups. • More time to practice and master concepts. • Social skills training and practice. • Kinesthetic and experiential group activities. • Guided choices. • Opportunities to experience short-term goal success. • Opportunities to use art and other creative expressions. • Connecting concepts with prior knowledge. • Structured learning. • Required reading materials below grade level, or limited in some way.
At Grade Level	• New embedded concepts without scaffolding. • Open-ended or unstructured group projects. • Unassisted learning of new concepts. • Materials that need to be read or are too far beyond grade level.	• Opportunities to practice without constant teacher input • Student-led activities and evaluations. • Guided choices. • Structured cooperative learning opportunities. • Chances to choose higher level learning activities. • Adherence to complete mastery of the grade-level standards.
Above Grade Level	• Activities from textbook or on grade-level materials. • Repetitious practice. • Teacher-talk lessons. • Expectations for mastery of grade-level objectives only. • Minutes wasted on grade-level activities and work sheets.	• Using resources beyond the textbook and other grade-level resources. • Opportunities to construct meaning. • Opportunities to go beyond the standard course of study. • Research-based projects. • Open-ended project choices. • Problem-based learning. • Compacting and individualizing.

Using Multiple Intelligences
to Help Students Choose Projects

You may not want to use Multiple Intelligences (MI) to group students, because there are so many of them. However, you may want to use it to design project choices, and students may need to know their strengths so that they might better choose which projects to do. Most likely they will be naturally drawn to projects that match their styles, but for planning purposes, you might want to know the number of students you have who represent each intelligence.

Although Harold Gardner's theory of Multiple Intelligences has not been explained by scientific research, his theory has been widely and successfully used by teachers who want to give students project choices based on a learning preference.

Lesson Idea Using MI

Here is a lesson you might use to determine students' strongest "intelligence."

Materials: Make "Intelligence Stations" around the room. Each station should have:

- *Verbal/Linguistic*: picture books, costumes, cloth, puppets
- *Mathematical/Logical*: rulers, calculators, math books, compass, protractor
- *Musical:* musical instruments, CD/tape player/recorder, microphone, cassette tape, CDs of various types of music
- *Bodily/Kinesthetic*: CD/tape player/recorder, CDs of various types of music, costumes, puppets
- *Spatial/visual*: crayons, colored pencils, clay, glitter, cloth
- *Naturalist*: string, nature items like pine cones, bark, leaves, stuffed animals, plants, etc.
- *Interpersonal:* dolls or puppets
- *Intrapersonal:* personal blank journals, mirrors

Station supplies: markers, posterboard and other types of paper, scissors, magazines; any group may respectfully borrow materials from another group if necessary.

Objective: Students will determine their strongest intelligence and teach the class about it by using that intelligence.

Instruction: Tell students you will be exploring how Gardner's MI applies to learning. Explain to them that they will be completing a survey that helps them determine an intelligence preference. Tell them that they may have other strong areas, but that one area may be strongest. If they have a tie for the dominant intelligence based on the survey, they may choose the one they like best for this class today.

Hand out this MI Checklist survey adapted from the Citizens Education Center.

Multiple Intelligences Checklist

Check all the statements that apply to you. The intelligence with the greatest number of checks is the one in which you are most strong. Note: You may have more than one strong intelligence.

Linguistic Intelligence

_____ Love to read

_____ Hear words in my head before I read, speak, or write them down.

_____ Enjoy language: the potential to excite, persuade, inform, or entertain.

_____ Enjoy reading or writing poetry.

_____ Excel in English and Language Arts.

_____ Conversations frequently revolve around things I've read.

_____ Enjoy word games like Scrabble.

_____ Enjoy doing crossword puzzles.

_____ Have written something recently of which I am proud.

_____ Total Checks

Logical–Mathematical Intelligence

_____ Can do mathematical operations in my head.

_____ Excel in math or science.

_____ Good at strategy games such as chess or checkers.

_____ Like to hypothesize and test my assumptions.

_____ Believe that most things have a rational explanation.

_____ Find logical flaws in things that people say and do.

_____ Will question persistently until I get an answer.

_____ Feel more comfortable when something is precise and can be measured.

_____ Total Checks

Visual–Spatial Intelligence

_____ Often see clear visual images when I close my eyes.

_____ Enjoy solving jigsaw puzzles.

_____ Have vivid dreams with clear images and colors.

_____ Can find my way around in unfamiliar territory.

_____ For me, geometry is easier than algebra.

_____ Can interpret two dimensional drawings.

_____ Like to construct models.

_____ Total Checks

Bodily Kinesthetic Intelligence

_____ Engage in sports, dance, or some other physical activity on a regular basis

_____ Find it difficult to sit still for long periods of time.

_____ Like working with my hands: sewing, weaving, carving, carpentry, model building, or some similar activity.

_____ Frequently use gestures, mime, and body language when conversing with someone.

_____ Need to touch things in order to learn more about them.

_____ Well coordinated.

_____ Need to practice a skill by doing it rather than reading about it or watching a video.

_____ Total Checks

Musical Intelligence

_____ Can tell when a musical note is off key.

_____ Frequently listen to music.

_____ Play a musical instrument.

_____ Can keep time to a piece of music.

_____ Know and like to sing many different songs or musical pieces.

_____ Can sing back songs I have heard once or twice.

_____ Repeat songs and tunes in my head.

_____ Often make tapping sounds or sing melodies while working, studying, or learning something new.

_____ Total Checks

Interpersonal Intelligence

_____ People come to me for advice or counsel.

_____ Prefer spending time with others rather than alone.

_____ Seek out others if I have a problem.

_____ Have many close friends.

_____ Prefer group sports or activities.

_____ Enjoy the challenge of teaching others.

_____ Consider myself a leader.

_____ Like to be involved in social activities.

_____ Total Checks

Intrapersonal Intelligence

_____ Need time alone to meditate, reflect, or think about important life questions.

_____ Seek opportunities for personal growth, i.e., to learn about myself.

_____ Have some important goals for my life that I think about on a regular basis.

_____ Have the will to carry out a project without much supervision.

_____ Can readily identify and express my own feelings.

_____ Have a strong sense of my inner self.

_____ Keep a diary or journal where I describe my feelings and values.

_____ Empathetic to the human condition and desire to make the world a better place through my actions.

_____ Total Checks

Naturalist Intelligence

_____ Love to be outdoors.

_____ Know how to identify most plants and animals.

_____ Would rather be hiking and exploring than just about anything else.

_____ Feel safe at home and in the woods.

_____ Know how to use a compass and most equipment useful for outdoor activities.

_____ Care passionately about the environment.

_____ Do well in science class.

_____ Total Checks

I have the most checks in the intelligence _____.

Name: _____ Date: _____

From A Personal Tour of Multiple Intelligences (1994).

Activity: As students complete the survey, they should go to the "Intelligence Station" that best fits them. They should then work with other students who are in this station to develop a presentation based on that intelligence that explains it to the class. Students may use the survey to give them ideas of concepts to show.

Student-Selected Groups

In the democratic differentiated classroom, at various times, students must be allowed to group themselves. This is a necessity if you are to dignify their ability to make good choices. One of the benefits of student-selected groups is that if you are asking them to extend learning beyond school, you may need to allow them to choose fellow group members with whom they might learn in their homes and communities. You would never assign a project that _required_ students to work together in their homes. That kind of assignment could make it impossible for some students to comply because of family and resources issues.

Additionally, if you allow students to choose their own groups, they can learn, sometimes the hard way, the perils of interdependency. If you choose their group, they might blame you if a group member does not do his/her part, but if _they_ choose their group, they can only hold themselves responsible. This responsibility for choosing fellow group members can teach students highly valuable lessons about trust and responsibility.

Personality-Based Groups

Learning styles aside, some students are simply more aggressive and talkative than others. Sometimes you might group students according to their dominance or shyness when it comes to class participation. If you put all the talkative ones together and the shy ones together, you will get interesting results. Often when the shyer students get a chance to talk, they show previously unknown leadership ability and intelligence. Unfortunately, sometimes, if all of the students in the group are similarly aggressive, they may get upset with each other, but this is a great learning experience for real world group problem solving.

Summary

In the democratic differentiated classroom, teachers may use various methods for grouping students for various types of learning. It is important to determine what kinds of groups: interests; learning styles; or readiness, self-selected, or personality based most closely match the learning activity. Having a democratic process in place will allow students to collaborate on how they are grouped; however, sometimes teachers may want to convince students that they should be grouped in ways that may not completely suit them.

5

Tools for
the Democratic
Differentiated Classroom

Matching Tasks to Learning Goals

10 Teaching "Tools"

Summary

In the democratic differentiated classroom teachers and students enjoy a variety of teaching strategies or tools within a framework of choices and a celebration of learning. These tools apply to democracy and differentiation because they offer choices: they allow students to determine their own reasonable level of difficulty and their own comfortable learning method, and they tap into students' personal interests. Because students are allowed these choices, they value and enjoy learning at high levels for its own sake. Teachers do not often need to make students do their work. This chapter presents "10 Tools" that you and your students may choose to use. Some of these tools come from others and some are those conceived or adapted by me. First, some thoughts about matching tasks to learning goals:

Matching Tasks to Learning Goals

- Teaching needs to match how the concept will be assessed.

  When choosing how to teach a concept, keep in mind how that concept might be assessed. For example, if you are teaching vocabulary words and your test asks students to write a definition of those words, then students need to practice doing that; but, if it asks students to choose the correct definition through multiple choice tests, then they need to practice learning the words that way.

- Use of deduction or induction needs to match how the concept will be assessed.

  Determining whether you will teach a concept through induction or deduction also depends on how you plan to assess the learning. For instance, if you teach students the definition of a word and then ask them to write that word in a sentence you are using a deductive process, but if you give the students a sentence that has the word in it and ask them to determine the definition from the context, you are asking them to use an inductive process.

- Instruction needs to match assessment methods imposed from outside the classroom.

  Choose how you will assess learning based on learning goals from within or from without. For example, often the state or local district decides for you how learning will be assessed. You need to teach students the skills they will need in order to achieve on mandatory state tests. You need to match your learning goals with that test. Most students will go along with this because they want to do well on these tests.

♦ Assessment methods need to match authentic students' needs.

Determine how you will assess a skill based on that skill's most authentic usefulness for students. For instance, if you are teaching the concept of developing a hypothesis in a science class, assess students' learning about developing a hypothesis by asking them to create and test a hypothesis. It might be less valuable to students to be able to identify the hypothesis in a scientific article. Even though teachers may expose students to excellent models of the use of hypotheses in real world journals, it may be more useful for students to practice the skill of developing their own.

♦ Creating an example or identifying an example needs to match the type of concept and the student competencies.

Whether you want students to create an example of a concept or to identify an example of that concept may depend on the concept itself and/or the learning competencies of the students (which you can determine through pretesting). For instance, I gave my students definitions of metaphor, simile, personification, and hyperbole. They were able to create examples of each of these terms; but, they could not correctly identify the terms when I gave them examples. Because I knew they would have to be able to identify these terms and understand their use in a work of literature, I provided learning experiences that allowed students to practice identifying as well as creating these terms.

10 Teaching "Tools"

After finding out how your students need to learn in the classroom, you need to have skills to develop a wide range of lessons that will reach all of your students. If you have taken time to learn about your students and asked them what they want to learn in your content area, you are ready to collaborate with them to meet their needs. In other words, you need to choose processes that match the content to the needs of each of your students. Here are 10 tools that closely match content to students' needs.

Tool 1: Building Background Knowledge through Sustained Silent Reading (Marzano)

One of the best suggestions I have come across in my research comes from Robert Marzano (2004) in his book *Building Background Knowledge for Academic Achievement*. Marzano's book provides teachers with two important ideas related to student achievement. The first is that improving students' background knowledge improves their achievement on standardized tests, and second, that background knowledge can be improved if teachers allow students to participate in sustained silent reading. Both concepts are enhanced if vocabulary is taught in a certain way. Marzano has advice based on considerable amounts of research about how to use sustained silent reading and how to teach vocabulary to improve student achievement.

A Five-Step Process for Sustained Silent Reading (pp. 46–61)

Step 1: Students identify topics that interest them.

Step 2: Student find reading materials associated with that topic.

Step 3: Teachers give students uninterrupted time to read.

Step 4: Students write or do something else associated with what they have read.

Step 5: Students interact with the information they have gained through reading.

Example: Using Sustained Silent Reading in Science Class

Step 1: Prepare: You are doing a unit on the human body (or an aspect of the human body). Ask your media specialist to make a display (a cart or table) with enough books related to this topic for everyone in your class to have choices of books to read. You may want to make sure you have multiple copies of some books if students want to work with a partner or in a small group. If your media resources are not large enough for this, form a partnership with your community library or other community resource. Make sure the book choices are in place before you take the students to view them. Before going to the media center to select books, preview some topics students may have an interest in. If possible, recommend some specific books to them. Do a "book talk" or get your media specialist to talk about some of the books. Pique students' interest in the various topics and the available books to read. Ask that students *think-pair-share* a topic in which they are interested. (Think-pair-share: Think of a topic, find a partner, share your idea with your partner.) Ask students to volunteer sharing their topic ideas with the whole class. This step gives students who are not sure about a topic more ideas from which to choose. At this point, your students will be eager to find a book that suits their interests. Note: If you have computers readily available, you may also extend this reading assignment to a certain number of online articles approved or suggested by the teacher. Or you might gather hard copy journal materials that may be acceptable. Students should be required to make an annotated list of these articles to address accountability.

Step 2: Students select the reading materials: *Important*—tell students in advance, how long they will have to read this book in your class. If you can only give them 15 minutes for two weeks, make sure to offer books they can read in that amount of time. Do not rely on students to read these books as homework. Students will self-select based on their understanding of their reading level. If you think your students do not know how to choose a book based on their comfortable reading level, teach them the *Five Finger Method*. (Five Finger Method: (1) Read a random page in the book you have chosen. (2) Each time you come to a word you do not know, hold up a finger. (3) If on that random page you run across five words you do not know (i.e., all five fingers are up at the end of the page), then the book is too hard for you.) Make sure everyone has chosen a book before leaving the media center. Tell students that as they find their materials, they should check them out and then sit down to begin reading quietly. Have an idea about how you will handle students' abandoning their first choice. Assure them that choosing another book is fine, but impress upon them that they need to make alternate choices quickly lest they fall behind.

Step 3: Within your schedule (60 or 90 minutes), you must find a time every day for students to read these books.

Step 4: Consider asking students to write a summary of what they've read each session (provide at least 5 minutes for this) or ask them to make an oral presentation each day. Ask students to keep a record of the words they do not know in their notebook. Depending on the age and level of your students you may want to have multiple or fewer checks on their reading progress. Use this rule: The younger and less skilled use more check-points, the older and more skilled use fewer check points.

Step 5: Make time for students to share what they have learned from the book that they have read. Allow students as much freedom as possible to decide how they will share the book with the class. In elementary or middle grades, students may want to work with a partner or small group to make presentations. Provide students with creative ideas for how to share their book. One of the best lists I've seen is called "75 Ways to Share a Book" by Suzanne Barchers. It is accessible online at http://mrcoward.com/slcusd/75.html. Some examples:

"1. Write about it to a friend.

2. Condense it to 15, 50, or 100 words.

3. List its 5 most interesting critical sentences.

4. Tell what the book would say about itself if it could talk.

5. Make a postcard out of it.

6. Become the author and tell why you wrote the book.

7. Do a cartoon strip based on the information in the book.

8. Rewrite it for a younger reader.

9. Write a song about it.

10. Create a mural about it."

There are many ways to make sharing a book creative and fun for all grade levels. This website is one of many that has suggestions that will help students make choices about how they might most enjoy presenting what they learned from their book.

Tool 2: Vocabulary Development: Characteristics of Effective Direct Vocabulary Instruction (Marzano, p. 90)

- Describe words instead of defining them.
- Use words *and* pictures to describe words.
- Gradually shape word meanings by exposing students to the word many times and in many contexts.
- Teach word parts.
- Use different kinds of instruction for different words.
- Use games to teach words.
- Focus on terms that are considered *most important* for academic achievement.

Marzano posits **6 steps to effective vocabulary instruction** (pp. 91–103):

Step 1: Teacher introduces the word and provides a description, explanation, or example of the new word.

Step 2: Students restate the explanation of the new word in their own words.

Step 3: Students create pictures or other nonlinguistic representations of the word. (They can act the word out in a kinesthetic skit.)

Step 4: Students revisit the word through activities that help them add to their knowledge of the word.

Step 5: Periodically students discuss the word with other students.

Step 6: Periodically students play games with the word.

Marzano's advice seems sound and easy to implement within various frameworks of curriculum design. The research suggests that the benefits of sustained reading and vocabulary development are substantial and difficult to refute. Reading and vocabulary development are important in every content area and at all three levels of instruction: elementary, middle, and high.

Example: Use Vocabulary Development in Math Class

Step 1: At the beginning of the year the math teacher determines a limited number of math vocabulary words that are critical to his math content area. These terms will be introduced as they appear in the curriculum. Students are asked to keep a "Math Vocabulary" notebook . When it is time to present the first math vocabulary word (or set of words that go together) to explain a mathematical process, the teacher asks students to explore that word or those words in great detail going beyond the textbook. The teacher should lead a discussion of the word or group of words in which he models for students how to explore a math vocabulary word. The teacher writes the first word on the board or overhead projector and around that word he and the class should come up with all or some of the following about the word: origin, synonyms, antonyms, examples, nonexamples, a definition, part of speech, use of the word in a sentence, pronunciation guide, and most importantly, a picture that represents the word in the students' minds. The teacher asks students to record this information in their notebooks.

Example:

Part	Whole
Less than one	
Definition:	An expression that indicates the quotient of two quantities, such as 1/2 From the Latin, *frangere*, to break
Word history:	Did not originally have a meaning in mathematics, was used to mean breaking or a breaking into pieces.
Noun	(Fraction)
	John gave Bill a small fraction of his money.
Frac' shun	Numerator over
	Denominator

Step 2: In a miniquiz at the beginning of class, ask students to explain the new word or words in their own words. Discuss the word or words again as a whole class. Show students how to apply the word in your math lesson.

Step 3: Differentiate so that *visual learners* make a two- or three-dimensional picture, *auditory learners* create and practice a verbal explanation, and *kinesthetic learners* plan a physical activity that represents the word "fraction." Students could do these activities on their own, with a partner, or in a small group.

Step 4: Students use the term *fraction* as they learn how to perform mathematical assignments related to fractions.

Step 5: At least three times during the unit, ask students to group themselves or get a partner to discuss their understanding of fractions. Have groups or partners share their discussion. You may want to practice these discussions so that you do not waste time. For instance, you may script the discussion through a series of questions about fractions that partners or groups answer together. Here are some suggested questions: How do people use fractions in real world problem solving? What is the most confusing part of dealing with fractions? How are the numerator and denominator related to one another? Etcetera.

Step 6: Ask students to find a partner or small group so that they might make up a game to play with fractions. Or you can go online and find a wealth of "Fraction Games" to play in your classroom.

Word (or Vocabulary) Diary

Here is a tool I developed that helps teachers prompt students to collect new words:

Step 1: Ask students to create a word diary by collecting words from content materials (chapters in books, short stories, math units). They may actually make a diary or just use a chart or double entry journal.

For example, they might say...

> Dear Diary,
>
> Today I learned these words:
>
> (1) manipulate: to change someone's mind.   (Define or describe)
>
> The nurse manipulated the soldier's wounded leg.
>
> (Write a sentence of your own.)

For each word, students write a definition or description of the word, write a sentence using the word, draw or paste in a picture that helps them remember the word, and others such as synonyms and antonyms.

Step 2: Tell students to make a test for themselves to evaluate their knowledge of the words they have collected. Their grades at this point can be counted or not.

Step 3: The teacher makes a test based on the words she determines are important in the materials the students have read. If a student did not collect one or more of the words, that meant they should have already known the word.

Imposing the idea that the teacher will test their knowledge of the words, students will be inspired to be diligent about gathering words they do not know.

Step 4: The teacher gives a unit test of the words and counts the grade.

Tool 3: Problem-Based Learning

Another wonderful strategy for engaging students in their own learning is the Problem-Based Learning (PBL) model. In their book, *Problems as Possibilities*, Torp and Sage (1998) explain that "problem-based learning is focused, experiential learning (minds on, hands-on) organized around the investigation of messy, real-world problems. It is both a *curriculum organizer* and *instructional strategy* ... PBL includes three main characteristics:

♦ Engages students as stakeholders in a problem situation.

♦ Organizes curriculum around this holistic problem, enabling student learning in relevant and connected ways.

♦ Creates a learning environment in which teachers coach student thinking and guide student inquiry, facilitating deeper levels of understanding." (p. 14)

Also, from Joel Greenberg (1990) we have the following definition of a "good" problem.

1. It requires students to make predictions that they can test.
2. It does not require fancy equipment.
3. It is complex and requires multiple strategies.
4. It benefits from group interaction.

In my *Handbook on Differentiated Instruction for Middle and High Schools* (2005), I provide the steps to design a problem-based unit. The steps include the following (pp. 160–162):

Step 1: Determine what goals or objectives you would like to achieve.

Step 2: Find a real world solution or create a situation that will require students to achieve your stated goals and skills.

Step 3: Ask yourself questions about the problem to make sure it addresses your learning goals.

Step 4: Decide how to present the situation to your students. Create a role, situation, and problem description.

Step 5: Present the situation to students, allow time for students to investigate solutions, hear their solutions, evaluate the solutions. (See Northey, 2005.)

If at first you are not comfortable designing your own problems, here are some sample problems that you might enjoy doing with your students.

PBL Sample Problems

This sample problem integrates Language Arts, Science, Social Studies, and Math. Note that each problem requires students to go through the six-step problem solving method. Refer to my book, *Handbook on Differentiating Instruction for Middle and High School* or go online and "Google" "six-step problem solving" to find several resources that describe this method.

Survival in Africa

During your Winter Break, your group is traveling to Johannesburg, South Africa on a Youth Peace Keeping Mission via a Cessna 185. You are half way to your destination when your pilot loses his radio and engine. Luckily, you were near a veldt on which to land the plane. Unfortunately, upon crash landing, the pilot is killed and all but one of you sustained injuries. One of you has a smashed patella. Additionally, you are in an extremely remote area where few people travel and the South African political situation has made search and rescue efforts questionable. What will you do?

Steps:

1. Students get into groups of fellow travelers on the airplane. As survivors of the crash, they need to go through the six-step problem-solving process to define the problem, examine challenges, and choose the best solution.

2. They must reach consensus as a group about what to do.

3. Next they write a problem-solution essay as a group. A team of teachers and administrators will score this essay (Level I, II, III, or IV). The essay should be hand written (rather than typed), and students should not put their names on it (for the purpose of anonymity).

4. Any information, materials, or supplies students bring into the scenario must be logical, probable, and possible.

Students' Health

According to studies, this is the first century in which the health of children in many cases is poorer than the health of their parents. Childhood obesity and other health related conditions are reaching frightening proportions. Adults are puzzled about why many students are unhealthy and they have done some things to address health issues. For example, the Health Department has noticed that students are purchasing fewer cartons of milk than they have in the past and they have designed a program to entice students to drink more milk. Nutritionists have called for better lunch choices in school cafeterias. Some policymakers have created laws that make physical education, or at least exercising, a mandatory, everyday event for students. There are many theories about why children as a group are in such bad shape, but only a few actual solutions to this devastating dilemma. What can a group of students at your school do to address this problem that threatens the future of our world.

Steps:

1. In groups of 4 or 5, go through the six-step problem-solving process to define the problem, examine challenges, and choose the best solution. Groups could be general or could represent simulated teams. You could group students by their preferred future career choices. For instance, you could have groups of doctors and other health care professionals, teachers, artists, service workers, farmers, etc. Or each group could be heterogeneous with representatives from various professions, such as, assign students to simulate teams that include at least one health care professional, one teacher, a parent, a business owner, policymaker, or other professions who might have a distinct perspective on students' health issues. Students would then use these various perspectives to help them look at the problem from several angles.

2. Each group should write a proposal for an action that might address students' health issues.

3. The class should choose the best idea, and then the whole class could work together to implement a plan for the school, the district, the community, or beyond.

4. Any information, materials, or supplies students bring into the scenario must be logical, probable, and possible.

Global Relationships

The world is shrinking because of vastly improved methods of communication and other technological advances. People can talk to other people across the globe as if they lived right next door; however, our world is not a peaceful place. Several cultures have resorted to terrorism to attempt to solve economic, political, religious, and/or social problems. In a world economy, problems arise as a result of our diverse methods of speaking, worshiping, and living day to day. What can be done to promote world peace?

Steps:

1. Each group (4 to 5 students) will represent a different country, such as: United States, European Union, Russia, China, India, Iran. Students must understand the political, social, and cultural identities of each of these countries in order to go through the six-step problem-solving process from the perspective of their assigned country.

2. Each group should write a proposal for an action that might address world peace.

3. The class should choose the best idea, and then the whole class will work together to implement a plan for the school, the district, the community, or beyond.

4. Any information, materials, or supplies you bring into the scenario must be logical, probable, and possible.

Schools

According to John Goodlad (2004), "American schools are in trouble. In fact, the problems of schooling are of such crippling proportions that many schools may not survive. It is possible that our entire public education system is nearing collapse. We will continue to have schools, no doubt, but the basis of their support and their relationships to families, communities, and states could be quite different from what we have known" (p. 1). Also, a recent news article stated that we are facing a "teacher shortage crisis." Are our schools failing their customers—students and their families? Are they also failing to attract teachers or keep the ones they do attract? What could a group of students do to save our schools?

Steps:

1. In groups of 4 to 5, go through the six-step problem-solving process to define the problem, examine challenges, and choose the best solution. Groups could be general or could represent simulated teams. You could

group students by their interests in the problem. For instance, you could have groups of teachers, parents, students, principals, policymakers, etc. Or each group could be heterogeneous with representatives from various professions. For instance you could assign students to simulate teams that include at least one teacher, a parent, a business owner, policymaker, or other professions who might have a distinct perspective on schools. Students would then use these various perspectives to help them look at the problem from several angles.

2. Each group should write a proposal for an action that might address the problem with schools.

3. The class should choose the best idea, and then the whole class could work together to implement a plan for the school, the district, the community, or beyond.

4. Any information, materials, or supplies students bring into the scenario must be logical, probable, and possible.

The Environment

Everyday we read or hear stories of damage being done to our earth. From global warming to the proliferation of deadly toxins, our world as we know it is in grave danger. Is anyone doing anything to stop this damage? Or has greed and ignorance doomed our planet to changes that may be irreversible if not stopped now. What can be done?

Note: You could use this over-arching problem statement or choose one that is specific to the area in which you live. The newspapers are filled with problem issues having to do with local environments.

Steps:

1. In groups of 4 to 5, go through the six-step problem-solving process to define the problem, examine challenges, and choose the best solution. Groups could be general or could represent simulated teams. You could group students by their interests in the problem. For instance, you could have groups of teachers, scientists, policymakers, business owners, etc. Or each group could be heterogeneous with representatives from various professions. For instance you could assign students to simulate teams that include each of the professions listed previously. Students would then use these various perspectives to help them look at the problem from several angles.

2. Each group should write a proposal for an action that might address the problem with the environment.

3. The class should choose the best idea, and then the whole class could work together to implement a plan for the school, the district, the community, or beyond.

4. Any information, materials, or supplies students bring into the scenario must be logical, probable, and possible.

New Teacher

You have just been hired as a teacher. You received the keys to your classroom that measures 30' x 36'. You have 26 students (per class if secondary) and 30 desks. You have a desk, a computer, a table for it, a file cabinet, two book cases that are 6' x 3' each, and a 4' round table with 4 chairs. Your principal has given you: 30 textbooks and other books in your content area, staplers, staples, Scotch tape, scissors, and other essential items. You have approximately $300. you can spend on supplies and equipment.

Students may work alone or with a partner to answer the following questions:

♦ How will you set up your room?
♦ What will the design of your bulletin board be?
♦ How will you spend your money?
♦ What will you do with your students the first day of school?

Have the following materials available: poster board, markers, rulers, scissors, string, glue, catalogues of teacher supplies, order forms, calculators, teaching ideas.

Students must turn in the following:

♦ A model of their classroom setup.
♦ A small poster that simulates a bulletin board.
♦ An order form that shows the supplies they plan to order with their $300. They should spend the money to as close to $300. (including tax) as possible.
♦ A lesson plan for the first day of school.

Teachers can plan their entire curriculum around problem-based learning, they can use one problem per unit, or they can use it one time in the school year. They can also investigate the Future Problem-Solving Program, by going online at www.frsp.org to find out more about this nonprofit educational organization. This organization has a catalog of resources for teachers who want to incorporate future problem-solving activities in their classrooms and it has a yearly future problem-solving contest that has Junior (grades 4–6), Middle (grades 7–9), and Senior (grades 10–12) Divisions.

Tool 4: Kinesthetic Ideas

As I said previously, any concept or lecture can be delivered via kinesthetic methods. Making abstract ideas concrete can help most students bridge the gap between confusion and mastery. Here are some creative ideas to address the kinesthetic learning channel.

Argumentation Skit: Starring Claim, Data, and Warrant

Actors:

1 Claim

3 Supporting Details (Data)

1 Warrant

The actors will act out the words of the narrator in an improvisational manner as the narrator speaks (with or without props).

Narrator: When you are writing to argue, you must include the following types of sentences: claims, supporting details (data), and warrants.

First, you must make claims that cleverly advance your argument. These claims must be strong and reasonable. They may also appeal to your reader's emotions.

Second, you must include sufficient details to support your claims. Your audience must understand and relate to your details so that you may reach "common ground" with them. Details must not make your audience angry so that they quit reading your argument and you lose it. *None* of your details should be off topic. They will weaken your argument.

Third, a very important sentence type is your Warrant. The Warrant must draw conclusions about your claims and details. Warrants must wrap things up neatly and be completely rational and convincing.

With these major sentence types in mind, you will make strong arguments that wow your audience and advance your argument to victory.

The End. (Thank the actors.)

Math Dramatics

Teachers can make up skits to teach concepts or they allow students to make up skits that help all learners learn new skills and/or knowledge. Here is an example of a skit I wrote to help students learn about mean, median, and mode.

Skit: "The Range"

Characters:

Detective (dressed in a trench coat etc.)

Ms. or Mr. Mean (dressed in cowboy clothes to look mean)

Ms. or Mr. Median (dressed in cowboy clothes to look average)

Ms. or Mr. Mode (dressed in cowboy clothes to look popular)

Setting: The Old West on "the range." Perform the skit at the white board. Draw some clouds in blue. Draw a tree on the left with a "0" on it and a fence on the other end with a "+9" on it. Make some green grass for the ground in between.

Detective (enters): Here we are at the scene of the crime. It happened here on "the range" between the numbers 0 and +9 (indicate the tree and the fence). A notorious gunslinger, Numbers Newman, was shot down in cold blood by one of the members of the Triple M gang. Here are our clues. Newman drew these numbers in the sand next to his body (write the numbers on the board 0 3 9 2 1 9 4) and he circled one number. I'm here today on the range to talk to members of the gang to see if I can get an idea about who might have committed this crime. Maybe you (points to class) can help me. Why here comes Mr. Mean now.

Mean (**enters**): Hello (in a gruff voice).

Detective: Hello Mr. Mean. I am here to interview members of your gang to try to solve the problem of what happened to Numbers Newman. Will you tell us where you were at the time of the murder?

Mean (**in a mean voice**): I might tell you, but I'm not going to help you solve the crime. I hated Numbers and I don't care that he is rotting in his grave. From my point of view, if you added up all his bad deeds and divided them by the number of people he hurt, you would know what I mean. I won't help you! (He exits.)

Detective: So if we added up the values of the numbers in the sand and divided them by the sum of those numbers, we would know if it was Mr. Mean who committed the crime. But wait. Here comes Median.

Median (**enters smiling and looking average**): Hello.

Detective: You must be Median. You're looking quite pleasant today. Can you help us solve the mystery of the death of Numbers Newman?

Median: I wish I could help you, but I'm just a middle of the road citizen with no special talents. I didn't like Numbers Newman, but his activities were none of my business. I don't have an opinion. I don't believe in one extreme or the other (indicates left and right); I just take the middle. I suggest you rearrange the numbers though if you want to know more about who killed him. Sorry I can't help you any more than that. (Exits)

Detective (**rearranges the numbers to show 0 1 2 3 4 9 9**): So, if the number Newman circled is the middle number … But wait, here comes Mr. Mode.

Mode (**enters looking too cool**): Howdy "pardner!" What ya'll doing out here on the range?

Detective: I'm here at the scene of the murder of Numbers Newman. Do you have any idea who killed him?

Mode: I am very popular as you probably know, but I don't have a clue who killed old Numbers Newman. I probably saw him more than any of the members of the Triple M gang because I'm "the Mode" (said boldly, with pride). I'm around more than other numbers. But I don't know who killed him. Good luck buddy! (Exits)

Detective: (Looks back at the numbers and thinks out loud). Let's see the numbers he drew were 0 1 2 3 4 9 9 and he circled the number 4. (Reporter circles the 4.) So who killed him?

(Enter *Mean, Median, and Mode,* simultaneously they do the following: Mean adds up the values of the numbers and divides by 7 in order to get 4. Median underlines the 3 that is the middle number and Mode underlines the two nines.)

Who dunnit? *Mean*

Tool 5: Choice

One of the most important aspects of the democratic differentiated classroom is offering student lots of choices, but sometimes students need some ideas to choose from. Having the projects categorized in terms of learning styles helps students add to their repertoire of assessment choices. Differentiated Project Choices is a project choice handout you may want to use when you assign an inquiry project.

Differentiated Project Choices

Each project should include a "Works Cited" page that includes at least 3 sources that informed your project. Please use the correct form. You will lose 10 points if you do not include this part of the project and if you do not correctly document your sources.

You may work by yourself or with partners.

Visual Learners

1. Make a book for an elementary student. The book should be based on the theme and have a minimum of 10 pages. Each page should include text and a picture.

2. Make a magazine based on the theme. The magazine should be laid out like a real magazine and have at least 10 pages of text and pictures.

3. Make a newspaper based on the theme. The newspaper should be laid out like a real newspaper and have at least 6 newspaper-size pages of text and pictures.

4. Make a PowerPoint presentation with at least 10 slides. Each slide should have text and pictures that relate to the theme.

5. Find or draw 10 pictures related to the theme. Write a paragraph for each picture explaining how the picture relates to the theme.

Auditory Learners

1. Create a CD or tapes of five songs based on the theme. The tunes may be original or borrowed. The words of the songs must be original.

2. Create an original book on tape related to the theme. The audience for the book should be elementary students.

3. Find five songs that are related to the theme. Explain why each song relates to the theme. You may print the lyrics and write why each song fits the theme (one half page minimum) or you could make a tape with each song and your explanation.

4. Record a radio show during which a host or DJ interviews "experts" and plays a song based on the theme.

5. Make a speech (live or on film) that addresses a major concern related to the theme. The speech should last about 3 minutes.

Kinesthetic Learners

1. Make a documentary or talk show related to the theme. The documentary or talk show should have an unbiased narrator and should make 5 main points through interviews or enactments. The documentary must last about 5 minutes.

2. Create an active game that expresses the theme. Write a brief explanation (one paragraph) about how the game teaches the class about the theme. Conduct the game in the class for about 5 minutes.

3. Choreograph and perform a dance that expresses the theme. Perform live or film the dance and provide a commentary explaining how the dance expresses the theme. You may provide the commentary in written form (one-half page) or tell about it at the beginning or end of the performance or film. The dance should last about 5 minutes.

4. Film or perform a skit or puppet show that clearly expresses the theme. The film or performance should last about 5 minutes. Provide a written copy of the script.

5. Make up a series of movements (e.g., cheers) that teach the class about the theme. Perform the movements or film them to show to the class. The performance or film should last about 5 minutes.

You will receive an extra credit grade if your project shows integration with another content area such as math, social studies, or science.

Tool 6: Inquiry Teams

Grouping students to do research is one of the most exciting strategies you might use in the democratic differentiated classroom. The team concept helps scaffold the idea of research because students can support each other in this somewhat complex process.

A word of caution, do not assume that your students know how to work in teams. Offer them guidance, for example, in the Inquiry Team Syllabus, the teams are asked to determine a voting method to reach consensus. Note: One of the best methods is to ask group members to point to the leader (they may point to themselves). The leader is the person with the most votes. This syllabus outlines the use of inquiry teams and an "Inquiry Team Project Grade Sheet":

Inquiry Team Syllabus

This syllabus can be used for inquiry in any content area.

Step 1, Planning: Meet with your assigned group to begin planning. Discuss your essential question and how you plan to report your answers to the class. Make sure each group member understands the requirements of the assignment as follows:

- ◆ A "Works Cited" page of at least 3 sources displayed in **correct form**. (Maximum of 5 points, one point per source.)
- ◆ A brief explanation of your process of investigation. (5 points)
- ◆ A visual support for your report (e.g., a poster, PowerPoint, or demonstration). The school provides some supplies, but you may want to get some things from home too. (20 points) Visual
- ◆ A hands-on activity to support your report. (20 points) Kinesthetic
- ◆ Reports must be timed to last no more than 15 minutes each. (You will lose points if your report has to be cut short because you ran out of time or because it is so brief that you are finished well before your time limit.) (20 points) Auditory
- ◆ Evidence that each member of the team was active in planning and implementation.

Suggestions for helping a group run smoothly:

- ◆ Elect a leader (with the pointing method).
- ◆ Break the assignment into parts and have each person responsible for a part.
- ◆ Plan a voting method to reach consensus on whose idea to follow.
- ◆ Let the teacher know if you are concerned about how the group is working.

Step 2, Inquiring: Find information to answer your question. Some suggestions for finding information:

- ◆ Go online.
- ◆ Go to the public library to get books beyond the scope of our school library.
- ◆ Interview adults who may be authorities on your topic. You should determine some interview questions prior to talking to an adult about the topic.
- ◆ Look in newspapers and magazines.
- ◆ Look in other content areas such as Science and Social Studies.

Step 3, Creating: Create your visual and your hands on activity. Visuals should be neat, creative, and accurate.

Checklist for PowerPoint presentations:

☐ 7 to 10 slides

☐ Text is meaningful and limited so that members of the audience can read all the words without having it read to them.

☐ Text is accurate with no conventions errors (i.e., misspelled words and grammar errors.)

☐ Pictures are relevant to the text.

Step 4, Practicing: Decide who does what and rehearse your presentation for timing. Sign up to present.

Step 5, Presenting: Each team member should have a role in presenting the report to the class.

Inquiry Team Project Grade Sheet

Team Members:

Grade Categories	Points Earned
1. Works cited (5 points) Comments:	_____
2. Explanation of research process (5 points) Comments:	_____
3. Visual support (20 points) Comments:	_____
4. Hands-on activity (20 points) Comments:	_____
5. Oral Report (20 points) Comments:	_____
6. Other (20 points) Comments:	_____
Total Points Comments:	_____

Tool 7: Extending Learning Beyond the Walls of the Classroom

Extending learning beyond the walls of the classroom can truly inspire students' involvement in learning at a high level. All you need is a body of knowledge, a method for determining territories, and some rules for students to get or lose points. You might use this kind of game with any body of knowledge. Here is an example of using it with vocabulary words.

Example Using Vocabulary Words
from any Content Area: Vocabulary War Games Rules

2 Teams: Green Team and White Team (use school colors)

Each team chooses a territory

Neutral territories:
- Any and all classrooms
- The main office
- Cafeteria
- Media center
- Car pickup area can rotate as a territory for both or all teams or be off limits. War zone territories: hallways

You may not run, participate in horseplay, or other immature actions. If anyone breaks this rule, the games are off permanently!

If you come across opponents in your territory, you may ask them to define a word or give them a definition and ask what the word is. You may only ask opponents to define words from units we have covered. You may only ask one word per encounter.

If they **do not know a word** one time, they are disabled. If they do not know a word a second time, they are out. You must tell your opponent if *you* are disabled or out. Once you are *out*, you are out of the game until we start again. We will start over each week with each new unit.

If they **know the word**, they get 2 points for their team. You get 1 point if you disable someone or put them out. Each team member must keep track of their own points.

Each team elects a **captain.** Team members report their points to the captain as often as necessary. You may take turns being captain if we continue the game for more than one week. The captain will keep a list of points earned on a card I supply.

The captain will **report the point totals on Wednesdays** when the game will start over.

The winning team gets 100 points as a vocabulary grade. The losing team gets 90 points as a vocabulary grade.

Tool 8: Small Seminar Groups

One of the cornerstones of a good democratic differentiated classroom is the seminar discussion group. Most teachers hold Socratic Seminars or Shared Inquiries in whole class discussions. You might consider breaking the larger group into smaller seminar groups. Here's how to do it:

Step 1: Divide your class into groups of 4 or 5.

Step 2: Assign all groups to read the same selection or chapter or article.

Step 3: Ask students to write a minimum of three open-ended discussion questions (you must teach this skill, see directions below). Or you might hand students a list of important questions you want them to answer orally.

Step 4: Tell students to elect a leader–recorder. This leader–recorder will track the number of comments made by each group member though the tallying method (‾H‾H‾H = 5). Teach students that all students should have a similar number of marks by their names so that the conversation will be balanced. Tell students they will be graded on the quantity and quality of their comments. The teacher must circulate and listen-in on the discussions to make sure students are staying on task and making high-quality remarks.

If you have developed a classroom culture in which students take responsibility for behaving responsibly and caring about the discussion, this kind of lesson works exceptionally well.

Step 5: When the teacher calls time, the leader–recorder should turn in the group tally sheets. Students should also turn in the questions they wrote for the discussion.

Students will enjoy the oral aspect of this type of lesson, but if you want to build in accountability, you might ask each recorder to record students' responses.

Step 6: You may want groups to report to the entire class any highlights of their conversations.

Tool 9: Double-Entry Journals

Another exceptional strategy is the double-entry journal. As students read any kind of material, they take notes organized into at least two columns. These journals can include words, sentences, pictures, thinking maps, and/or questions that help them recall what they are learning and that help them categorize what they are reading. Any time you can get students to make reading more kinesthetic (taking notes), you help them understand and remember what they have read in any content area. Students could make these journals on their own, in groups, or with a partner.

Here is an overview of possible journal assignments:

Abstract	Concrete
Word	Definition
Question	Answer
Math Concept	Example

Tool 10: The One-Minute Speech

This last tool is lots of fun and can be used for any content. After students have learned content information through research or through other inquiry, assign the one-minute speech as follows:

Step 1: Students develop a topic or learn about a topic.

Step 2: Give students index cards and tell them to summarize the topic information on the card to help them plan their one-minute speech on that topic.

Step 3: Use the consensus rubric (see the example in Chapter 3, p. 56) to determine how students will be evaluated on their speeches.

Step 4: Give everyone in the class small pieces of paper on which they will write their evaluative feedback for each student.

Step 4: Use an overhead timer to time students as they speak.

Step 5: Ask the audience to write the speakers' names on the small pieces of paper and then to write feedback to give to the speaker on that small piece of paper.

Step 6: Have a student collect the feedback notes and give them to each speaker.

Step 7: The teacher also gives students feedback on their speech. Below is a sample feedback form.

Speech Feedback Form

Name:	Date:	
Categories	*Maximum Points*	*Actual Points*
Sticking to time limit	50	
Speaking distinctly and audibly	20	
Speaking with conviction	20	
Developing a charismatic relationship with audience	10	
Total	100	
Comments:		

The final aspect of this chapter is a template that provides an overview of planning a democratic differentiated unit.

How to Develop a Democratic Differentiated Unit

Theme-Choosing Meeting

- Teacher provides list of themes.
- Students choose theme in democratic fashion (majority rules) see Chapter 3, p. 41, for instructions on how to run this meeting.

KWL Session (p. 42)

- Teacher brainstorms with students to determine what they already know about the theme.
- Students pose essential questions. They also think about skills, knowledge, assessment products, and learning activities.
- Students and teacher decide how students will learn about the theme. Teacher and students may plan separately at this point.
- Teacher gives students a Project Proposal form (see Chapter 3, p. 43, for explanation) to help guide students in the planning process.

Teacher	Students
1. Examine the Standard Course of Study (SCOS) to determine necessary skills and knowledge that fit with the theme.	1. Think about how interests fit with the theme.
2. Determine skills, knowledge, and attitudes that might be explored in various learning activities.	2. Determine skills, knowledge, and attitudes that might be explored through various learning activities.
3. Determine acceptable evidence of learning	3. Determine how to present knowledge and skills to teacher and class.
4. Find materials that relate to the theme and that support the skills, knowledge, and attitudes that relate to the theme and to the SCOS.	4. Find sources that relate to the theme and that support the skills, knowledge, and attitudes that relate to the theme and to the SCOS.
5. Plan activities that will teach these skills, knowledge, and attitudes and that will address the big idea and essential questions for the theme.	5. Plan activities to do in class and at home that will address the big idea and essential questions for the theme.

Collaboration and Feedback

Teacher and students come back together at this point. Students share their proposals with the teacher to get her input. Teacher shares her learning plans with students to get their input.

Assessment, Evaluation, and Reflection

Teacher evaluates students' products and performance in meeting the goals that both have set. Students evaluate their own products and performances and give feedback to their peers about their products and performances. Teacher and students reflect on the successful and less successful aspects of the unit.

Summary

The tips I have listed are organic to democratic and differentiated instruction; all have been used successfully in my classroom. I use many other tools, but those presented in this book are the most successful for use across content areas.

If you want to create a democratic differentiated classroom, you should have a solid knowledge of the strategies that align well with students' needs. Many more strategies can be found in my *Handbook on Differentiating Instruction for Middle and High School* (Northey, 2005). Note that the democratic differentiated classroom aligns well with "Assertive Discipline" ideas and other enlightened discipline methods that ask students to share the classroom responsibility with the teachers. In my book *The Four Most Baffling Challenges for Teachers and How to Solve Them* (Waterman, 2006), I provide an overview of discipline and motivational methods that are also aligned with the democratic differentiated classroom.

References

Action Research. Retrieved February 13, 2006, from http://www.scu.eud.au/schools/gcm/ar/whatisar.html.

A personal tour of multiple intelligences. (1994). Seattle, WA: Citizens Education Center.

Barchers, S. *75 Ways to Share a Book.* Retrieved June 16, 2006, from http://mrcoward.com/slcusd/75.html.

Bloom, B. S. (Ed.), Englehart, M. D., Furst, E. J., Hill, W. H., & Krathwohl, D. R. (1956). *Taxonomy of educational objectives: Handbook I: Cognitive domain.* New York: David McKay.

Brooks, J. G., & Brooks, M. (1993). *The Case for constructivist classrooms.* Alexandria, VA: Association for Supervision and Curriculum Development.

Butler, K. A. (1987). Successful learning strategies for the emerging adolescent. *Oklahoma Middle Education Association Journal*, (pp. 1–7).

Catpin Resources. Retrieved May 12, 2006, from http://www,catpin.org "Chapter Three: 2005 Mathematics Objectives." *National Assessment of Educational Progress.* Retrieved December 4, 2005, from http://www.nagb.org/pub/m_framework_ 05/chap3.html.

Covey, S. Jr. (1998). *The seven habits of effective teens.* New York: Fireside.

Deci, E. L. (1995). *Why we do what we do: Understanding self-motivation.* New York: Penquin Books.

Dewey, J. (1916). *Democracy and education: An introduction to the philosophy of education.* New York: The Free Press.

Erickson, H. L. (2002). *Concept-based curriculum and instruction: Teaching beyond the facts.* Thousand Oaks, CA: Corwin Press, Inc.

Fauré, G. (1887). Pavane. *The most relaxing classical album in the world...ever!* (CD) Virgin Records America, Inc. (1997).

Fogarty, R. (1995). *Best practices for the learner-centered classroom.* Arlington Heights, Il: Skylight.

Gardner, H. (1983). *Frames of mind: The theory of multiple intelligences.* New York: Basic Books.

Gardner, H. (1993). *Multiple intelligences: The theory in practice.* New York: Basic Books.

Goodlad, J. I. (2004). *A place called school.* New York: McGraw-Hill.

Greenberg, J. (1990). *Problem-solving situations.* (Vol. 1). Corvalis, OR: Grapevine Publications, Inc.

Gregorc, A. F., & Butler, K. A. (1984, April). Learning is a matter of style. *Vocational Education 59*, (3), 27–29.

Gregorc Associates. (1999–2004). Retrieved June 3, 2004, from http://www.gregorc.com. *"History" National Assessment of Educational Progress*. Retrieved December 4, 2005, from http://www.nagb.org/pubs/history_06.doc.

Jensen, E. (1998). *Teaching with the brain in mind*. Alexandria, VA: Association for Supervision and Curriculum Development.

Jung, C. (1933). *Modern man in search of a soul*. Orlando, FL: Harcourt.

Kathy Schrock's Guide for Educators. Retrieved May 16, 2006, from http://schooldiscovery.com/schrockguide/assess.html.

Kolb Learning Styles. Retrieved May 15, 2006, from http://www.businessballs.com/kolblearningstyles.htm.

Kuhn, T. (1962). *The structure of scientific revolutions*. Chicago, IL: University of Chicago Press.

Maker, J. (1996). *Nurturing giftedness in young children*. Arlington, VA: Council for Exceptional Children.

Marzano, R. J. (2004). *Building background knowledge for academic achievement*. Alexandria, VA: Association for Supervision and Curriculum Development.

Marzano's New Taxonomy. *Intel Education*. Retrieved February 5, 2006, from http://www97.intel.com/en/ProjectDesign/ThinkingSkills/ThinkingFrameworks/Marzano.

McCarthy, B. (1981, 1982). *The 4 mat system: Teaching and learning styles with right/left mode techniques*. Wauconda, IL: About Learning.

Midlink Magazine Teacher Tools. Retrieved May 16, 2006, from http://www.ncsu.edu/midlink/ho.html.

Myers, E. & Rust, F. Eds. (2003). *Taking Action with Teacher Research*. Portsmouth, NH: Heinemann.

Myers, I. B., & McCaulley, M. H. (1985). *Manual: A guide to the development and uses of Myers-Briggs type indicator*. Palo Alto, CA: Consulting Psychologists Press.

National Research Council. (1999). *How people learn: Bridging research and practice*. Washington, DC: National Academy Press.

NC Standard Course of Study. Retrieved June 6, 2006, from http://www.ncpublicschools.org/curriculum/languagearts/scos/2004/23grade6.

Nelson, J. (1996). *Positive discipline*. New York: Ballantine Books.

Northey, S. S. (2005). *Handbook on Differentiated Instruction for middle and high school*. Larchmont, NY: Eye On Education.

O'Brien, L. (1990). *Learning channels: Preference checklist*. Philadelphia: Research for Better Schools.

Pellegrino, J. W., Chudowsky, N., & Glaser, R. (Eds.). (2001). *Knowing what students know: The science and design of educational assessment*. Washington, DC: National Academy Press.

Piaget, J., & Inhelder, B. (1969, 1971). *The psychology of the child.* New York: Basic Books.

Rozsa, Miklós, Eadie, Rack, and the Victory Symphony Orchestra. *The film music of Miklós Rozsa: The Jungle Book, Spellbound [soundtrack].* (CD) Pearl (May 21, 1996).

Rubistar. Retrieved May 16, 2006, from http://Rubistar.4teachers.org.

Silver, H. F., Strong, R. W., & Perini, M. J. (2000). *So each may learn: Integrating learning styles and multiple intelligences.* Alexandria, VA: Association for Curriculum and Supervision Development.

Skills and Competencies Needed to Succeed in Today's Workplace. Retrieved June 24, 2006, from http://www.ncrel.org/sdrs/areas/issues/methods/assment/as7 scans.htm.

Sternberg, R. J. (1997). *Thinking styles.* New York: Cambridge University Press.

Synectics... Retrieved February 4, 2006, from http://edweb.sdsu.edu/ Courses/ET650_OnLine/MAPPS/Seynectics.html.

TeAchnology: The Web Portal for Educators. Retrieved May 16, 2006, from http://www.teachnology.com/.

The Kennedys. *Angel fire* (CD). Philo/Pgd. (1998).

Tomlinson, C. (1995). *How to differentiate instruction in the mixed ability classroom.* Alexandria, VA: Association for Supervision and Curriculum Development.

Torp, L., & Sage, S. (1998). *Problems as possibilities: Problem-based learning for k-12 education.* Alexandria, VA: Association for Supervision and Curriculum Development.

Trussell-Cullen, A. (1998). *Assessment: In the learner-centered classroom.* Carlsbad, CA: Dominie Press, Inc.

Waterman, S. S. (2006). *The four most baffling challenges for teachers and how to solve them.* Larchmont, NY: Eye On Education.

Wiggins, G., & McTighe, J. (1998). *Understanding by design.* Alexandria, VA: Association for Supervision and Curriculum Development.